UNTIL WE KNEW, TWICE: LIFE WITH MND/ALS AND FTD

ELISABET O KLINT

UNTIL WE KNEW, TWICE: LIFE WITH MND/ALS AND FTD

This edition published in 2023
By Foxridge & Camberbatch,
An imprint of The Black Spring Press Group
(Eyewear Publishing Ltd)
London, United Kingdom

Translation by Margaret Myers
Cover design by Andrew Magee
Typeset by Subash Raghu

ISBN 978-1-915406-99-6

www.blackspringpressgroup.com

FOREWORD

The first thing we noticed was that his speech deteriorated. He had difficulties with words themselves, getting them out, saying them. That was at the beginning of 2015. When I brought this subject up with my husband, he said that, yes, it was true: 'I find it hard to speak from time to time.' That was when our life started changing, and we began the long journey to a diagnosis, and then yet another diagnosis. ALS (amyotrophic lateral sclerosis) with a bulbar onset (mouth and/or throat region) together with FTD (frontotemporal dementia). A ferocious combination. Very unusual and nasty – with a predictable, but at the same time unpredictable, progression. Dementia transforms a person, and social filters cease to operate. This affects how a person behaves, what he says and what he does.

My husband took a drastic decision by suddenly leaving me and our son. He chose another new and exciting way of life. He chose to have two homes. In the spring of 2016, we didn't know that he was incurably ill and didn't even know that such illnesses existed. My attempts to hurry along a visit to the doctor were met with delay and Mats did not want to seize hold of the situation; his view was that his symptoms were caused by stress. Our GP agreed with him on this for a very long time, although I myself never believed it. In the summer of 2016, his speech got worse and worse and he had more and more problems with phlegm secretion. At last, Mats was remitted to an ear, nose and throat specialist. At that point, everything accelerated and it was then that I realised that this was something really serious. Mats may have realised the same thing, but perhaps he did not as yet.

In September and December 2016, the result arrived, or the results. Our life as we knew it was pulled away from under us and another life started. A new everyday life with two incurable illnesses that had aggressive courses. It was rapid. More rapid than anyone could have predicted. It took turns that scared me and turns that demanded my love, my care and all my strength. My beloved husband was admirable in so many ways. For him, the only focus was on finding a cure, on living his life, doing all the things he usually did and also all the new things now being added. His need for human warmth, closeness and security dominated and my deepest hope is that he felt that he was held in their embrace and could experience the love that I could give him.

On 12 October 2017, his life faded away. Grief came later, over how things had been and how they had turned out, the agony of anguish, memories of inadequacy, and insights into how life follows its own path. How unable we are to control everything, however much we desire to do so. How love can exist in the midst of all this when it has in fact waned and lost its footing — just when we needed it and each other most of all.

What I have chosen to write has been written as my diary, but retrospectively. I wrote it to work through the grief that gripped me more than I was prepared for. It struck me hard and immediately just after the funeral, as I have heard can be the case. I had no choice but to try and help myself, and this I did by clothing my thoughts and feelings in words so that I could see them, look at what had happened to us and read about it. I wept and wept tears of despair. Writing this hurt, but mostly did me good, becoming my medication and therapy. Now I have a story that will endure forever, one that is true and that will be a kind of reminiscence of our final years together.

The word I write is sometimes *illness*, sometimes *illnesses*. When I write about it as one illness, I mean ALS. That was the illness that Mats talked about, took in and was totally aware that he had. Frontotemporal dementia (FTD) was something completely different. It was an illness that he never mentioned – and I believe that was because he never experienced himself as having it, or perhaps could not understand how it changed and destroyed him. However, the dementia was obvious and very here and now for me, particularly during the second half of his period of illness.

My hope is that this diary can help other people; my words, thoughts and feelings side by side with everything that actually happened. The facts as they were in our case. It isn't an attempt to describe what it's like to live with, and in the middle of, diagnoses like these in the general sense – but only to share how things were for me, how things were for us. Our experience of how our life together challenged us before it suddenly came to an end. Expected but unexpected, and nobody saw it coming. Neither I myself nor the care team.

March 2020

*My diary about
loss, love, grief and adjustment*

This diary is written retrospectively between 4th December 2017 and 5th March 2018, after Mats passed away. You can find the timeline, in chronological order, from first symptoms to death on page 250.

4 DECEMBER 2017

Now that the funeral is over, I'm inwardly dazed and in a dizzy mess. I'm confused by everything and can find no peace anywhere. A new life is beginning, with a situation that I couldn't ever have imagined. I want to escape from anguish and the painful memories of how things turned out – that my husband should have been struck down by two incurable illnesses that destroyed him both physically and mentally. Diagnoses that I had never even heard of before then, happily unaware of a fate that can strike anybody, at any time – MND, motor neurone disease, or ALS, amyotrophic lateral sclerosis, which is the term used in Sweden. In the USA, they sometimes use the term Lou Gehrig's disease, after the famous professional baseball player with that name.

Before Mats died, our contact with the medical services was comprehensive – including plans we had for him and needs that I voiced more and more loudly so as to get help with them. There were the never-ending thoughts about the illnesses and how I could give him support while at the same time preparing myself for the next phase, the next deterioration. Continual deterioration is the norm and what one must live with.

There are cases, about 15%, in which an unusual form of dementia develops in connection with the ALS. Sometimes it has its onset first, sometimes there are later onsets – frontotemporal dementia: *'up to 15% develop frontotemporal dementia'* (1). And it turned out to be that tragic – his fate was to end up in that group. I have read a great deal about this: *'patients with this diagnosis usually experience a rapid decline in both physical and cognitive abilities. The course of ALS with frontotemporal degeneration may run as quickly as 2 to 3 years, as opposed to the 5 to 10-year course more commonly seen for other forms of FTD.'* (2)

Looking out of the big, beautiful windows in our flat in Sweden feels pleasant and all wrong at one and the same time. Here was I on my summer visit and I had just started to consider the idea of moving home to Sweden after twenty years. Lovely England that I had so enjoyed and always been fond of long before we moved there as a family. Mats' great dream and plan to live in that country that he felt to be his own, where everything they did was right. Historical pride with the world as reality. To live in the English countryside in a fine old house with a long history was what he had mapped out and had as his plan for us. How quiet it is here compared with England, none of the small talk that I like so much and have a greater need of than ever.

The home I must now get used to living in is mine – it never became ours, other than on paper. I can see him thriving here, beside the sea and in the southern Swedish province of Skåne that he so admired. It was probably the proximity to Denmark, and the similarity to England with all the country estates and manor houses. How lovely it is here, with newly sanded floors, the rooms freshly painted and our furniture in place. Yet the feeling of sitting in the luxury of one's own residence, spacious for two and now even more so just for me, is not a genuine feeling of joy in my heart. Only my brain is assuring me that this was the right decision – at the time when we took it. I see how delightful the view is, the sea, trees and houses nearby. I marvel at all we have jointly gathered together during our life together. It is lonely and strange. More permanent than I feel at all ready for. In England, we never owned our home – the prices would go down and we were going to wait until one day soon!

5 DECEMBER 2017

I awoke with that feeling of vacuum rendered by grief, and my thoughts returned to the funeral. Light and beautiful, family, relatives and all our wonderful friends who were there. The vicar's words were neutral but warm; I had wondered a good deal about what he was going to say about Mats' and my life together. It turned out well, it was in any case honest, which was so important to me.

It surprised me that I was so focused and collected at that moment. I remember almost everything. Even the minutes before the bells started tolling; it felt like a long time to wait at that point. But it felt comfortable that time seemed to stand still. I had listened to the music time and again, and knew that it was right, for me and the children. And also in Mats' taste. The parts in English were special, and important to us since we had felt so at home there. Also because that included our friends who had travelled from there to be with us and to say farewell to their British-Swedish friend. The words were in tune with my view of love as changing throughout life, with the difficulties experienced together affecting it – and us.

Now my husband has many places in my home. Photos in frames, all of them my choices. He enjoyed seeing himself in photos and in this way the focus that he always directed towards himself manifested itself here as well. However, I made my choices for my own sake, to have the side of him that I want to be present in my life, now alone, as a widow who has just recently moved back to her home country.

A strong, healthy man with ambitious goals took us out into Europe while a gravely and incurably ill man brought us back to Sweden. The latter was a must, a shared initiative taken in agreement. A choice so that we would have more help with all that was to come, be close to family and old good friends during the time that he still had on his side. That I thought that he still had on his side. Life offers no answers in advance, and if I had suspected that the situation would change so suddenly, drastically and unexpectedly, the idea and plan to move back home would never have cropped up. But we had no idea. And I was in panic, panic and fear over how the illnesses changed him so aggressively. Especially during the summer of 2017.

Frontotemporal dementia is much less common than other types of dementia and often has different early symptoms. This means FTD can be hard for doctors to diagnose as they may not recognise its symptoms as dementia. Most changes in behaviour or personality caused by FTD may not be very obvious at first. These kinds of symptoms – for example, risk-taking, loss of social or sexual inhibitions, or obsessive behaviour – can sometimes look more like the person is going through a difficult or emotionally-challenging time. The first noticeable symptoms for a person with FTD will be changes to their personality and behaviour and/or difficulties with language. (3)

It was no longer possible to reason, discuss and plan, or to know what he was thinking or guess how he might act. And act he did. He committed

a crime and then our reality became quite
another from his just being ill. That reality I
share with my children, and only my children.
The consequences, and the extent of how pow-
erless we became from that moment, are hard to
explain. What happened gave me insight into
how his illnesses affected life for us too, especially for me as his wife and responsible carer.
And in the midst of the hell we were already in,
with its depths of anxiety, despair and grief, we
as a family suffered an even worse crisis.

Mats' anguish over what he had done was
obvious to me, and I still suffer to think of how
he got himself into the situation that arose. How
did it happen? Was he provoked and did he go
mad with all the thoughts that he was completely unable to control, or was he obsessed by
a certain person?

We will never have an answer to these questions. However, the helplessness that entered
into our lives at this point will always exist
inside me as a reminder of how a healthy and
ambitious person can become a prisoner of his
own reality when his brain is being destroyed.

Beloved Mats, how it torments me to produce these memories of you. How I wish that I could have come even closer to you in your fate and in your despair. I promise you I did everything I could to sort this out, solve it and help you. It took time before you were calmer, time before you could let go of your fear that the police would come back and arrest you. It was terrible for us all.

The policeman who caught you red-handed must have realised at once that you were very ill, but just not how ill. You could not speak, and you were hardly even able to make yourself understood in writing. The collapse and destruction of your language is something I have often sat looking at – the texts and e-mails of your last three or four months of life were almost completely unintelligible. Absolutely so for anyone who had not been accompanying you on the whole journey.

Remembering this will never allow me total peace, but it will give me a form of acceptance and insight into how alone you were even in our midst.

6 DECEMBER 2017

Of good and well-meaning advice I received plenty. All the responsibility lands in one's lap as the closest relationship and nobody around one has anything like the same kind of reality and everyday life to cope with. 'You have to get him to stop driving the car!' And how do I do that? Throw away the keys or actually sell the cars? 'You have to get a power of attorney, take over the responsibility for your shared finances and be able to take decisions on medical issues if he is unable himself to decide what is best for him.' And how do I explain and relay this to a clever man who has had (and still to some extent has) a grasp of all this? He was never easy to influence. For me at any rate, and for the children. To explain all the legal aspects of the purchase of the flat in Sweden, which was something positive that he wanted, was difficult enough. Sometimes it was as though we were three plus one, that one having the veto. All this is included in and part of what I am grieving over. Why did it turn out like that when our love had been so strong?

We had tons of things that were fabulously good; we were very fortunate. We had our children as we wanted, healthy and happy. They were able to grow up in a secure home, a security to which we both contributed. We were also healthy of course – and his career launched us out onto gorgeous adventures, with opportunities for moving to other countries. Exciting and with chances to expand our horizons.

I am so grateful that it became our reality, and I often think of it as something that we must value. Achieving one's goals. The love for and attraction to England existed in us both before we met, and was a strong link between us.

'I've done everything I wanted to,' he often said. For a long time it made me glad when I heard that, and I thought that it must be such a good feeling to have about one's life and one's situation in it. He helped himself to what he wanted, both in making the career that he chose and was suited to, and in his leisure time that he was careful to put to good use. He did precisely what suited him, things that offered challenges and satisfaction: riding, hunting, mountaineering, hiking and taking care of the garden. Being out of doors, where he was at his best, happiest and calmest, not least.

Later on, my understanding of that statement changed. 'I've done everything I wanted to' acquired another meaning for me. It no longer made me happy, simply pleased for him, or secure, knowing that was exactly what he felt. It felt painful instead, after the diagnoses had been decided in the autumn of 2016. Because now I knew that his life was about to come to an end, that was a fact. What chance did I have, or what chance did the children have, of being an important part of having 'done everything I wanted to'? The words were his about his life, with us slightly to one side, like a permanent anchor. He was in the outer lane, forever in the process of overtaking, making his own priorities and winning. Was I an anchor for him? Someone who held the boat still and offered calm, while he rode the waves on the ocean? Did we exist in his dreams about his life?

7 DECEMBER 2017

When did he actually fall ill? Did it make any difference, was I important, or more important, when he was ill? He lost words, but he did say 'I love you' anyway, every day, in a way he had not done when he had his health. Did he feel panic, did he believe I would fail him? He knew quite clearly that I could have chosen to do that. Quite justified and normal according to the rules in a marriage and a permanent relationship. However, I did not make that choice, and that was at least as much my saving as it was his. Being there at his side right up until the moment he drew his last breath was natural and even a privilege – a means for me to find peace and happiness in a life that I know is fragile. It can change, and also be taken from us, in the mere blink of an eye.

I wonder when he realised that he really was seriously ill. I think a lot about what his thoughts must have been that summer, 2016. All those visits to the doctor. For me it meant anxiety, anger and confusion when he chose to 'check out' – temporarily, as he said. He must have known, or at any rate suspected, that something was wrong. His speech was very badly affected all that year. It was during August, I believe, that he realised what a hellish situation he was in, and when he got hold of all available information, using all his strength and will. Without talking to me.

Some months earlier, in February, he suddenly got his mobile phone out and turned it towards me to show me something. It showed photos from a small flat and he told me as though it were self-evident that he was going to live there for a while. I understood nothing. Nonetheless, a couple of weeks later, he moved in there. We were supposed to be testing what it was like to be away from each other. He would come home often, and then we would discuss money matters and other practical subjects. What was the matter with him? How could he just do that, without any kind of discussion or dialogue? He decided this entirely on his own behind my back, and the time and place fitted

in perfectly with his polo-playing. Like a kind
of summer holiday accommodation.

*Frontotemporal dementia is often confused
with depression, occupational burnout or other
mental illness. Falling ill involves a slow transformation of personality, and the ill person
behaves inadequately or wrongheadedly more
and more often. The capacity to feel empathy
gradually deteriorates. The symptoms of frontotemporal dementia vary according to where
the brain damage occurs. It usually happens
in the frontal lobe that otherwise steers our
concentration, judgement and impulse control
among other things.*

*Deteriorating initiative capacity and flex-
ibility are other early signs, as are sudden and
apparently inexplicable outbursts of anger.
The person often becomes apathetic, restless,
self-absorbed and emotionally blunted. The
symptoms increase in number and seriousness
as the brain damage spreads.*

*The illness can be difficult to discover since
forgetfulness, learning difficulties and other*

typical symptoms of dementia are unusual at the beginning of the course of the illness. The symptoms generally appear to creep on as they do in Alzheimer's disease. On the other hand, the memory and learning capacity seem most often not to be affected to the same degree in frontotemporal dementia. Frontotemporal dementia is also known as frontal lobe dementia. (4)

8 DECEMBER 2017

I tried to persuade Mats to go to the doctor right from the time when his speech started tripping over itself. He found it difficult sometimes to get the words out, but his speech was normal in between times. Shortly after our house-warming party in our new house, I noticed that he could not always get hold of the words for what he wanted to say. I heard how he battled with this when he spoke to clients and colleagues on his mobile. And then his speech could be completely distinct the next minute. And so it continued to change back and forth. The first visit to the doctor was in the autumn of 2015 – several months after we had talked about his difficulties now and then in being able to get out what he wanted to say. However, the spring and summer took all his attention, because then the polo season was in progress and everything else was less important.

When he returned from his visit to our General Practitioner (GP), he said that she, like himself, believed that his speech difficulties were stress-related. I wanted him to take up the fact that his father had suffered a stroke in middle age. He had recovered quite well from that, but I thought that stroke might be hereditary. Was his speech affected by a stroke, or a tumour? This was how I brooded, believing that it was a TIA (Transient Ischaemic Attack – a temporary lack of oxygen in the brain's blood vessels that soon passed) or a brain tumour that affected and impaired his speech.

I felt an acute need to have answers to my questions since I was beginning to suspect that something quite serious was behind the symptoms. Mats had never had any problems with his speech when he was stressed, and he had certainly been stressed before. However, it was quite clear that he had no influence over his own health in this case, although he was a person who drove his life forward with such focus and decisiveness. Always had a plan, structure, boundless energy and stamina until he was finished and had reached his goal. But not with this.

ALS is an illness that successively breaks down the motor nerve system. This breaking down causes the voluntary muscles in the body to weaken and atrophy. The first symptoms often begin as a weakness in a leg, an arm or a hand. Muscular weakness can for example make it difficult to keep one's balance when walking up or down stairs, or to open tins or put a key in a lock. For some, the symptoms start as a weakness in the tongue or throat. This can make it difficult to speak or swallow. In due course, most people with ALS find it hard to walk, swallow and speak. People with this illness also lose weight since ALS causes their muscles to atrophy. In some, the personality and behaviour are affected on account of the damage to the nervous system. Gradually, the respiratory muscles get weakened, making it hard to breathe. Respiratory difficulties are usually what leads to death. Patients with the most serious forms of ALS die within a couple of years of falling ill. Some may live for ten years or longer with the illness. (5)

My anxiety grew and I took over. I searched for the names of neurologists because I thought that an MRI scan (Magnetic Resonance Imaging) ought to be carried out. I booked it privately and he went there alone at the beginning of February 2016. He did not want me to accompany him. Nor did he the time after that. Odd. The images showed that everything was looking normal, a healthy brain. When he came home after that visit, he was relieved – and who would not have been? Fantastic that everything was in order. He told me this and also that they – he and the doctor – had had interesting discussions about the EU.

But what was it that was affecting his speech then? I would have put that question if I had been allowed to be there. That Mats did not is something that I can see as human – getting away as fast as possible, relieved that his brain was healthy. Who would want to continue digging around in it? When one is told that one is healthy although one has gone around worrying that one might be ill. So nothing happened for a while.

It is difficult to make the ALS diagnosis since there is no one specific test to confirm it. In its initial course, the symptoms can resemble those found in other illnesses. Investigations must therefore be carried out first, to rule out all other, more treatable illnesses like stroke and brain tumours. Unfortunately, this involves taking a long time to make the diagnosis. ALS can be hereditary, but most often there is no explanation for the illness.

9 DECEMBER 2017

Yet another polo season took over our lives, and all attention was focused on that. By then, the problem of phlegm secretion became more evident than previously. He kept coughing and clearing his throat. Back to the GP again. Antibiotics were prescribed on two or three occasions, I think. Finally, at last, he was referred to an ear, nose and throat (ENT) specialist. Privately, of course, if it was to be done at once. That is how things work in England and it is surely the same slow process in Sweden. Nothing happens automatically.

The ENT doctor was the key to things picking up speed. He saw from Mats' tongue that something was wrong, neurologically speaking. And after that he wrote a referral to yet another neurologist. I was not allowed to accompany him on these visits either. Mats simply informed me. When he told me about the first visit that was approaching a diagnosis, he was not worried. He just said what the doctor had stated: 'It's something to do with your nerves.' My comment was chilly: 'Then it must be your physical nerves, not your mental ones,' I said. That was the only way I was able to express that I did not believe one single bit that it was stress that was the cause.

I was frustrated and angry on account of everything that had happened, and everything that he had not let me share. I was quite simply damned tired of the stress theory. The theory that had gone so far that the GP had sent a referral to the hospital's speech therapist as early as the autumn of 2015 and only much, much later to the ENT specialist. The referral to a speech therapist was given only routine priority and since that department had a high volume of referrals, the waiting time was estimated to be 16 weeks. A referral to a neurologist seems never to have existed in the minds of the doctors at the local healthcare centre. It was the phlegm secretion that led to a referral, based on the theory that it was an infection.

10 DECEMBER 2017

The day that the diagnosis was confirmed is one that I remember in detail, up until the point we left the hospital afterwards. An awful day, grey and dark, Monday 19 September 2016 at 3.30 p.m. In the morning, an engineer from BT had arrived to install SKY. I remember his face, his comments and how we reasoned about what he said about all the technical stuff. It wouldn't work, he said, unless we did a mass of extra manipulations that seemed taken from another world at that moment. Just leave it. We skipped the lot. At 3.30 p.m., Mats had an appointment with the professor of neurology at the hospital. We had lunch at home and the words he said when he got up from the table were these, for ever etched in my memory: 'Today I'll be learning my fate.' Those were his precise words.

I can point out which parking space we occupied, where we sat in the waiting-room and I recall distinctly what it looked like when the professor came out and called us in. He introduced himself and also two young women, both medical students. He asked whether Mats would agree to their being present. 'Yes', he said, and 'No', I thought. We sat down with the desk between us and the doctor, with the young women slightly to one side. Mats was examined and medical terms flew round the room. Education for the women. It felt degrading that our tragedy was to be a necessary part of their training. They had not even completed their education, and we became a suitable example of how a diagnosis of premature death may be received. I could have screamed (and still can) at how wrong this was. Then Mats could cover his upper body again with his clothes and come back to the desk. Then came the words. The words that will never fade. Mats was asked the question: 'Did Doctor A tell you what you have?' I was still of the belief that this was a second opinion. 'No', was the answer. But perhaps he did know, perhaps the other neurologist had said more than he was able to take in. I was not there on that occasion either and did not know exactly on which date he had been there, but probably at the end of August/beginning of September. 'It is motor neurone disease, a very serious and life-shortening condition.' That was what he said to us, word for word.

Did Mats know or suspect that it was anything as devastating? He just sat there and received it in silence. I cried. He had taken care of everything without my being there. Up until that visit, two weeks earlier, on 7 September. That was to a lung specialist, another referral related to the problem of phlegm secretion since the antibiotics had not made any difference. That day was the first time that I sat at his side during a visit to a doctor. Which is what I had wanted to do all along, but not been allowed to.

The cause behind ALS is unknown. There are many different hypotheses. One hypothesis is that there is too much of the signal substance glutamate in the brain and that it damages the nerve cells. The medication that exists works by inhibiting the release of glutamate enabling the cells to live longer. Virus infections, heavy

metal poisoning and a deficiency of trace ele-
ments are some of the factors being studied by
researchers. In the USA, ALS is called 'Lou
Gehrig's disease' after Lou Gehrig, a well-
known baseball-player who contracted ALS.
Many others with ALS have been physically
active. Studies have therefore been conducted
to see if a high level of physical activity may
lead to this illness. None of them have been
able to confirm this, however. (6)

On 7 September 2016, I suddenly became
invaluable to my husband, and since that point
in time, I was the only one who really seemed to
mean a lot to him. It was a pretty sharp about-
turn.

He begged me to accompany him and
beamed with happiness when we met outside the little hospital. There he stood in his
white polo clothes, with his arms outstretched
towards me. He must have known already that
he had been afflicted by something serious. And
also realised, if only deep in his soul, that it was
hell, real bloody hell.

All those visits on his own, when he had sat alone (I think) in the waiting-room and in doctors' surgeries and barely been able to make himself understood. The pain of sitting there with him, but also the calm and security of being able to be there that late summer day, when with my own eyes I saw how totally vulnerable he was. So dependent that somebody just must help him. I was angry and I was troubled. He was still living in his temporary summer hideaway and was probably suffering terribly from what he had done, the decision he had taken some months earlier. Back then in February, when neither of us knew that his stumbling speech was the beginning of the end. When he wanted to live his life without me, but nevertheless still have me in the background. While another woman filled his vision in the foreground.

I do not believe that Mats experienced his transformation or that his behaviour was abnormal. Nothing in his communication intimated that he was worrying about how he was living or behaving. He chose whatever attracted him most when it suited him and never expressed any worry for the future. When one has FTD one can perhaps not understand – or even understand that one does not understand – what one is doing or why. Or that the person one has become has such a strong effect on others. Especially how those closest to one are 'afflicted' and have to take an enormous responsibility. The patient seems to have no insight at all into the illness.

The frontal lobes have a control function the purpose of which is to make us aware of the consequences of our actions, and that our choices are significant. The illness puts that function out of action, as though the individual has been given blinkers and considers themselves as the most important person with a single goal in life: to achieve immediate satisfaction. What develops out of this is egocentricity.

11 DECEMBER 2017

The letter from the specialist arrived the day after the appointment with her, 7th September, according to normal routine of following up with a written report to both the patient and the GP concerned. Mats received his letter in his e-mail. He forwarded it to me and asked me to print it out. Not a word of shock, fear or worry about the contents of the letter.

The sentence a little way down in the text read: 'My biggest concern would be motor neuron disease.' I googled it and cried out aloud when I read the paragraph that appeared on the screen. I got into a total panic, tears coursed down my face and I ran to the telephone and rang one of my closest girlfriends, a nurse. She listened and tried to calm me down. She told me not to continue reading, but instead to wait until we could speak to a doctor. I knew absolutely nothing about this disease. I knew who Stephen Hawking was, but could not have said which illness he was suffering from. I knew of *the ice bucket challenge*, but the name of the illness to which it was to draw attention was one I had never memorised. The creator of The Ice Bucket Challenge was the baseball-player Pete Frates, who received the diagnosis ALS in 2012. He decided that it would be the beginning of his struggle, not the end of his life. Many people, both famous and unknown, were filmed when they poured icy water over themselves.

Amyotrophic lateral sclerosis, ALS, is a disease that attacks the motor nerve cells (the ones that steer the muscles' movements) in the brain and spinal cord. First the nerve cells are damaged, and then they are gradually destroyed. The person affected experiences this nerve damage through the atrophying of the muscles and resulting paralysis. Since it is only the motor nerve cells that are affected, consciousness is not affected.

It is not only the motor nerve cells in the brain and upper part of the spinal cord that are affected, but also those in the lower part of the spinal cord. The upper and lower damages result in different symptoms, and these symptoms together are thus characteristic for ALS. The symptoms of upper motor neurone damage are stiffness (spasticity), muscle twitching and muscular shaking (chronic cramp). The symptoms of lower motor neurone damage are muscular weakness and atrophying. These types of damage are often shown by ALS patients as for example uneven/mincing walking, stumbling and falling over, loss of muscular control and strength in hands and arms, difficulties in talking, swallowing and breathing, chronic tiredness, muscular twitching and cramps. (7)

12 DECEMBER 2017

Mats wanted to have a wedding ring. The one he had was never any good, so it had not been on his finger for at least twenty years. I took off my rings when I knew how he had betrayed me. He pointed to his finger and said that he wanted me to put on my rings again. I often think about all the thoughts he must have had about how he had handled his life, and how often he had neglected me and the children in favour of his own focus and his own interests.

It must have been chaos inside him at that point, with the despair of wishing he could turn back the clock. He wanted us to be the couple that he actually had as his dream, somewhere in his heart. With the needs he had now, in the present. A symbol like the rings probably felt important. Did he want to make even more sure that I would always be there for him, and with him, considering all that he was unable to do? And everything that was to come. Did he know what was to come? Had he read about the phases and the course of the disease, did he understand – and in that case could he take it in?

ALS patients deteriorate over time and it becomes harder and harder for them to move, talk, swallow, and breathe. Various aids are required to help give nourishment and medication, and a ventilator is needed to alleviate respiratory difficulties. The respiratory muscles become afflicted, with symptoms like fatigue and powerlessness as consequences. Carbon dioxide is no longer breathed out in a normal way and the cause of death is most often 'carbon dioxide narcosis', or else pneumonia.

13 DECEMBER 2017

Only a week after the ALS diagnosis, Mats started reading about and seeking information on research projects. Driven, as in everything else he did, this now became his daily business. Who could even think of questioning that? How is one supposed to deal with one's death sentence when healthcare has nothing to offer as a cure, nothing to suggest even that might make a difference? For ALS specialists it must be a routine matter more or less, breaking this news to people, and what I heard between the words was roughly: 'Go home now and make the best you can of the time you have left.' How do you do that? A suggestion from the perspective of a healthy person, it seems logical just to enjoy, get as much as possible out of the good things in life. Can people do that when standing eye to eye with death? Does the truth not weigh you down all the time, the reality and uncertainty about the time left? The knowledge about the course of the disease

– your body gradually shutting down, speech becoming impossible, difficulties in swallowing and finally, the attack on your breathing. With normal thoughts? – if frontotemporal dementia is not part of the diagnosis?

What the patient notices with ALS is a weakness that starts somewhere, often in a hand or a foot. At first one does not understand what it is. It does not strike one suddenly, but successively. One gets more and more clumsy, drops things, trips for example over the edge of a rug. When the patient is aware of these effects, then it is estimated that about 80% of the nerve cells have already been destroyed. The illness begins long before the patient feels any symptoms, perhaps a year earlier. We do not know exactly when it starts, since we do not know the cause of the disease. Regardless of which form the illness takes at first, weakness spreads in the body. The deterioration happens gradually and at an even speed to the point when the muscular atrophy finally affects the breathing. In certain patients, there are tendencies towards cognitive impact, certain impact on personality that may for example show itself in the form of what is known as emotional lability. Patients may suddenly become very emotional and start weeping, for example.

The progression of the disease means that weakness spreads in the body. In the end, it affects the muscles that enable us to breathe, that is, the diaphragm. It is a large muscle that separates the chest cavity from the abdomen. When it no longer functions as it should, then breathing stops functioning. It is not the lungs that are defective, but the muscles that enable us to breathe in that are affected. The end point of the disease is reached when that happens and that is what causes the patient to die of ALS. (8)

There were two research projects that Mats focused on, and he searched for all information available on these projects. He obviously wanted to be included in them and saw them as treatment, not just as research trials. I told him what I knew about research on ALS; I was able to think realistically and knew that one might end up in the control group. One must match the project and cannot even decide oneself if one is to participate. The research team does that, based on the specifics of their research – age, how long one has had one's diagnosis, what type of diagnosis it is and so on. And, with frontotemporal dementia, the situation, and his possibility for inclusion were different.

However, I realised that talking like this was meaningless. He worked with such focus, and this was a new obstacle that he was just going to conquer. He was used to getting his own way, to leading others and setting out goals – taking what he wanted and arguing his way forward in life. The same was valid now and it was just a case of stringing along. And this was the saving of his mental stability, I believe. If he was in the driving seat, he felt at home. 'Fuck the doctors', he often said, 'they do nothing.' He expressed himself in English more and more often to me. He gesticulated with his hands to show his anger and lack of respect for the doctors who were taking care of him. He expressed hate and extreme frustration.

14 DECEMBER 2017

He wanted a second chance to be examined. Would I have been able to accept the facts if I had been given his diagnosis? In our case, there was one big obstacle specifically, and that was the dementia. Could somebody be accepted who was not clear about all the things to be decided before signing his name as part of a research project? Medical ethics are central. Dementia puts a stop to it, if it is not dementia in particular that the research is about.

I was given advice by a friend who knew about certain things from her contacts with the field of pharmaceuticals. She mentioned something called the *compassionate use programme*. It involves access to unregistered medications that can be prescribed for humanitarian reasons. I took this up with the professors, but I did not get a real hearing from them and my question was never followed up. Perhaps there was no such medicine involved in ALS research? Nevertheless, I believe it depended on the dementia.

It had not yet been confirmed, but the suspicion existed in the mind of the professor from the first meeting with Mats, and perhaps even before that. I am sure of it, and I have my reasons for that.

15 DECEMBER 2017

From the diagnosis and onwards I started to pray to God: 'Take Mats while he can still walk.' I repeated this time and time again. It was my greatest terror with ALS – that I would have to see him suffer as paralysed, without the possibility of enjoying the curative powers of nature and the freedom to go for walks. Everyone wants this, and he did not need it any more than anyone else, and with respect to our differences this is always the case. But he was an enormously physical person: army ranger, horseman, skier, mountaineer and hiker with an insatiable need for physical fatigue and exhaustion. Not to speak of the mental kick it gave him to deal with and conquer dangerous situations – adrenaline kicks. To be the best, to win and demonstrate his strength. Not least to himself. This was his most distinctive characteristic.

His brain was always working at full speed, and therefore needed the help of a tired body –

a body that wore out and quietened the motor in his head, always in top gear, never in neutral. The military years had shaped him, I think, and created a lifestyle that was forever part of him. 'Take Mats before he becomes paralysed', again and again this was my prayer. His speech was more and more difficult to understand, steps on the path towards later becoming silent, not being able to swallow and then not being able to breathe. With that prognosis, one has to make the best of today. And where was the forum for support and hope within healthcare, while we were slowly approaching the inevitable? Hope combined with ethics, naturally, not quackery. The latter existed in the periphery as the doctors had warned us.

I was so close to Mats and he was physically as close to me as he could possibly get. I became his only and great security, in my embrace with his arms around me was where he wanted to be, so close that there was no space for me – that space was taken up by his desire for belonging and human warmth, and his aspiration to stay alive.

Witnessing and experiencing this, and continuing to give, despite anguish and feeling divided in myself, is the greatest agony I have ever met. It is this that I must do my best to process, I must give it a place inside me and ease my judgement of how everything turned out. Was I the best I could be to give him everything that he so frantically sought after? Did he feel a sense of security in what I most of all wanted to give, my forgiveness?

16 DECEMBER 2017

When we were done at the private hospital on 7 September, and Mats had been given an appointment for a lung X-ray, we went our separate ways. I went to my job at the university, and he to play a polo match. It was warm and lovely and we were still happily ignorant. He had on his white polo jeans and a blue polo shirt. He was handsome and suntanned. When I arrived home that evening, he came in when passing, driving to his new temporary flat, the one he had so much wanted to move into a few months earlier. Where he would stay to have a break from me that happened to coincide with the polo season – when life was like a game to him. When the Argentinians came back to England, with their horses and the whole team. He had a new season with matches and tournaments before him.

He popped in, and I clearly perceived that something was different compared with other times he had come home to us to talk. I had had the same feeling at the hospital earlier that day.

He had sat so close to me in the waiting-room, gone and fetched water for me, it was very stuffy. It was as though he was begging on his bare knees – look after me, help me, forgive me, let me come back and be with you all the time.

When we had talked for a while, he took the remote control in his hand, I shall never forget it, and was just about to turn on the TV, as though he were going to stay. Then I said: 'Now you should be going, shouldn't you?' Then he put back the remote as though he had already decided himself that he was not going to stay. But I know, I know with absolute certainty that the only thing he wanted was to stay there with me and creep close to me that night and conjure away the hell that he had caused. His adventure, a so-called agreed time apart, fuelled by his lust and his own interests – and fuelled by what I now believe, even know, was a damaged brain affected by frontotemporal dementia. I did not know then that it even existed. One only ever hears about Alzheimer's.

When we stood there at the front door, I felt deeply how painful it all was. I suffered with him, although I was still both angry and confused over how he had betrayed me and our children. The pain of seeing him walk to his car, the desire to hold him to me and beg him to stay, these are feelings I can relive when thinking about that occasion. I wept in despair as soon as he had left, the tears were impossible to stop that evening and night. I was upset to see him so desperately alone, upset over my own suffering and the knowledge that something must be seriously wrong.

Sometimes I wish that I had said: 'Stay here, come and sleep by my side.' So safe we would have felt together. But I did not feel confident, not just then, and my feelings and my anger had to be allowed to exist. They were my reality and my pain and I was battling with them. He had done so much harm and my reaction was natural. I just could not ask him to come back, and to stay with me. I am also a human being with needs and feelings, with integrity and the right to be angry, disappointed and deeply affected.

17 DECEMBER 2017

Twelve days later, we would know, on 19 September. During those days, between 7 and 19 September, I wrestled with Mats' anguish in wanting to come back to me. He seemed to love me more than ever. He had decided to quit his temporary flat – without discussing it with me. He only wanted to be with me. I was at my wits' end. Despite this, it took no time at all to make the only decision I could. To take him back into my life, look after him and allow him to return home.

In a conversation with my psychologist, almost one year after his death, she summarised in writing a little of what we had talked about:

> We talked about guilt being a normal part of the grief process. It's experienced by those who didn't have the relationship complications that you had. You recalled barely having time to process the relationship issues before you were having to face the devastating news of Mats'

illness. I think at that point you may have entered some type of survival mode. Just to get through the illness as best you could, doing the best you could with what you had. This leading to you having to suppress many of your more painful emotions and vulnerabilities – in order to self-protect. The man who had betrayed you was also dying in front of your eyes. As I write this Elisabet I feel your pain, your dilemma so acutely and I wonder and admire how you got through this. He was certainly well cared for and advocated for by you. You were there in so many important ways for him. Try to focus on what you did – not what you didn't do.

18 DECEMBER 2017

What do you think about when you get a diagnosis like ALS? How much do you take in? I cannot rid myself of this thought. What has he actually struggled with, what did he know, what was he most afraid of? How lonely did he feel? How much did he regret that he did not take care of us, me and the children, during his final years? Or perhaps he did not regret anything at all? He was completely engulfed by other things that interested him, other people who seemed to mean so much more. Also by another woman. A love affair and relationship that was eventually exposed. A person who was there as well as us. For how long? Was he even able to think about himself in those terms? About what he had done; or was he already lost in his own world, in a radically changed brain?

Why did he fall ill? What causes people to get ALS, and frontotemporal dementia? There are genetic explanations in about 10 percent of cases, but all the others are designated as sporadic (isolated) cases of ALS. Sometimes ALS brings with it other illnesses, most often frontotemporal dementia.

Is it something chemical in our surroundings, something he did in the military, or just chance? Had there been accidents in which he was injured that have triggered the illnesses? He had fallen off horses, pushed himself to extremes in the military and taken risks in various sports. He was always naturally lean. For a few years (midlife crisis) he avoided potatoes and bread, and that soon showed on his waistline. Was that a good thing? And later on, his damned eagerness and desire always to be best, doing everything possible before a competition – he had to win at any cost. Was there a risk in this that could lead to developing ALS? There are several examples of elite sportsmen and high achievers who have been afflicted by the illness. Lou Gehrig is one. Pete Frates another.

Exposure to lifestyle and environmental factors that might contribute to the development of MND has been extensively studied over the years. This research is known as epidemiology. Epidemiological studies have identified possible links with prior exposure to mechanical and/or electrical trauma, military service, smoking, agricultural chemicals, high levels of physical activity, and a variety of heavy metals. However, it is important to note that these are only suspected contributory risk factors and the evidence obtained in these studies has often not been conclusive. (9)

I put some questions to the professor on that occasion when I was searching for information on dementia, paralysis and the prognosis in terms of time. He said then something about high achievers, a category to which Mats definitely belonged. But the scientists do not know for sure. Was there a link to ten years of military work? He was a military man to his fingertips. And the extreme physical pressure of playing polo at a higher and higher level? We human beings are designed like a Volvo, but want to perform like a Porsche, was one thing the professor mentioned. If that is true of anyone then it was certainly true of Mats.

When I finally knew for sure that dementia was a fact, the pieces of the puzzle fell into place, thinking back a couple of years. The professor was of the opinion that FTD appeared first in Mats' case. I am convinced that if that was the case, perhaps it even appeared as early as 2013. Definitely 2014. His sporadically odd behaviour lacked a distinguishable line of progress, or a wholeness. That was why there was no warning for us. It is not until you know that you can see it clearly in the rear-view mirror. Only a few weeks after he had been diagnosed with ALS, the professor said 'I think there are other cognitive problems', and he wanted to ask a clinical psychologist for an assessment in order to confirm or be able to dismiss his suspicions. I believe that he knew already. 'Do you make financial decisions?' he asked Mats. 'Maybe you should get involved', he said to me. 'Have you got power of attorney?' was another question. What's that? I thought. Guardian? The healthcare authorities wanted me to consider making medical and economic decisions for Mats. All these well-meaning pieces of advice and comments on what should be done in the middle of a situation that was already chaotic, complicated and emotional, and anything but simple.

I had helped the professor by writing a letter to the neurologist Dr A, who was the one who actually made the ALS diagnosis and then referred us to the MND team at the university hospital. I wrote that letter after the milestone visit to the doctor when I was allowed to accompany Mats for the first time. It was the lung specialist's words: 'my greatest concern would be motor neurone disease', that naturally made me write to neurologist number two, Dr A.

19 DECEMBER 2017

At that point, Mats' condition had deteriorated so much that I was in despair, thinking what might be wrong with him. It made me see how necessary it was to tell some doctor or other how he had chosen to live since a while back. How he had changed and that I did not know what it was that was driving his worrying behaviour.

When Dr A wrote her verdict, that was sent to Mats on about 2 September 2016, she must already have been sure of the diagnosis ALS, and perhaps even have said it to him during his visit. Or did she want the hospital's experts in neurology to be the messengers since that was where one belonged during the time one was living with the disease? Instead of telling Mats herself, and explaining exactly how gravely ill he was. Or had she informed him?

I realised without a doubt that it must be something critical since she had expressed herself in this way in her letter: 'I strongly suggest that you bring your wife with you to the appointment…' That is to say, the visit to the hospital on 19 September. That was why I wrote to her. With complete openness, I told her about everything that had happened since 2015. That letter has been included in Mats' medical journal. It must in some way have raised a warning flag for the professor at the hospital; that a change in behaviour, with spontaneously and drastically made decisions, was possibly a sign of dementia related to ALS.

Here is an excerpt from the letter that I wrote to the neurologist who probably made the diagnosis, who remitted Mats to the MND clinic where the professor confirmed the diagnosis in September 2016.

Dear Dr A,

I'm writing to you about my husband, Mats […], who has seen many different doctors and consultants since the beginning of this year. In spring 2015 I started to notice his difficulties articulating and getting words out […].

I was concerned that he should see a neurologist and knew this would be very slow through the NHS and I therefore booked it privately in January. The MRI scan was normal and no further investigations done. Mats and the GP seemed focused on stress as a possible cause [...]. He has also been treated for sinus/chest problems with antibiotics [...]. I want to explain why I haven't been welcome to join Mats at any of these consultations [...].

Yours sincerely

And here is an excerpt from the doctor's reply, dated from the middle of September:

Thank you very much for your letter which was very helpful. Thank you for being so frank. I was concerned about what I was finding on examination and wanted to ensure that you were present at the next consultation. It sounds like it has been a truly awful year

[…]. I am very sorry for what you are going through.

Yours sincerely

20 DECEMBER 2017

Conversations with a psychologist have been a great support for me. She is my psychologist thanks to the MND team. She works with patients who have been afflicted by some neurological disease or other and with relatives to find out how they are affected. The first month after the diagnosis, I read about the disease. Then it was impossible to continue doing so. I suffered unbelievable anguish from knowing what the course of that hellish disease was going to be.

Different, but nonetheless the same, I think. What always happens is that towards the end one cannot swallow and then one cannot breathe. Regardless of whether one has become paralysed first, that is always how it ends. Not everyone gets paralysed, however. That one question out of the three I asked in October 2016, in connection with the suspicion of dementia: paralysis, prognosis, and dementia. I had to know more.

So an appointment was made for me with the professor. I wanted to be alone. And my first question was: are there cases in which one does not become paralysed? 'Yes, it can happen but it is very unusual.' That ignited a tiny hope in me. Think if Mats was unusual? The prognosis was 'around two years' – impossible to know exactly, but one asks anyway. And then I also had questions about dementia and the consequences if that were to be confirmed. The risk was apparently great that he might also have dementia.

It is like having a poisonous snake wriggling around in your body while you are still feeling as you usually do. Now I knew enough, could not cope with taking in any more – did not want to know any more, quite simply. I was unable to be active in the local MND association either, despite their wooing us with letters. They meant well, of course. But it was enough that we had this in our lives every day as it was. It was enough that I saw what I saw in the waiting-room at the hospital. Meeting others with the same or a similar fate would only increase my anguish and Mats was absolutely not interested.

The few moments that I had to myself were needed to replenish my energy and find a little joy in life, not to fill up instead with more illness. With all respect for others who see things differently and seek for links to other families with the same tough reality and everyday situation in life. Though for me, I knew that it would break me down while I was in the midst of everything, instead of creating strength and a sense of community. Or being able to ease our everyday life in some other way.

It was enough to be with Mats in everything that now dominated our life. Nothing was at all positive, no hope of a cure or any kind of improvement. It was all about mapping out the course of the illness until the end arrived, giving the best possible support medically and personally. At the same time, I knew that one day I would want to belong to that group – to give and receive along with others who understand completely.

The meetings with my psychologist were invaluable. She gave me a lifeline and I do not know how anyone could manage without that support. I wish that we had recorded our conversations, so that I could have listened whenever I have the need. Her balanced suggestions, in which she took both our sides, were useful to me. She never left Mats out of our conversations.

She was deeply knowledgeable about how others had lived and were living in the same situation, and deeply insightful about what Mats' world was like, medically and mentally. Our whole family was included in these conversations, even though I was the only one of us present there. She put a great deal of emphasis on how I was to look after myself. Taught me a technique for handling my panic attacks – which I had never experienced previously in my life. They were awful. The body's physical reactions resemble certain illnesses.

She knew everything about us, because I chose to give the whole picture and background, so that I would be able to receive better support. I could just have fled away when the diagnosis was made. I had not chosen to be discarded, but discarded I was without any discussion. He chose to keep us at a distance, to live a free life with horses and new adventures. Self-centred, drastic and strange.

21 DECEMBER 2017

Now, afterwards, I know that this may be a behavioural disturbance caused by FTD. Not the unfaithfulness of course. But leaving suddenly in the way he did is not the decision or actions of a healthy human being. I know who she is. I was there when Mats met her the first time. Two couples at the same wedding who happened to be seated at the same table. In June 2014.

However, that piece of the jigsaw did not turn up until much later, two years later to be exact. When somebody decided to give me and the children the news in an e-mail with information, detailed information. The aim was to injure our whole family. That succeeded. At the same time, it presented the image of an unpleasant type of personality. This knowledge was of help to me one year later in connection with the crime that Mats had committed and the contact I was thereby compelled to have with the police, in July and August 2017.

Now that I have the whole picture before me, I can also see many other signs of dementia. The way he got stuck on one track, one theme, one thread in a discussion. His anger against the EU became a continual subject of conversation. Like a damaged gramophone record. Also his wanting me to read something specific in the daily paper. Every day for a long period of time, text in articles was highlighted in colour to show me what I ought to know. This was a pattern during the whole of his period of illness, that everything important was highlighted: names, dates, figures, times, items in a list.

Long before his speech was affected, Mats had a routine that we all noticed and wondered about rather, but no more than that. He was completely caught up in the film *Frozen*. It had appeared in 2013 and he watched it again and again in 2014 and 2015. We laughed at it some-times and wondered what it could be that was so gripping. We laughed and he laughed with us. Of course it must have been the dementia that took him to a world in which the capacity to assess what was enough had atrophied.

As a healthy person, he had been a romantic who liked films like *The Sound of Music* – films with elements of the military and love, or of social classes, as in the musical *My Fair Lady*. Did that contribute to the fact that we did not see his obsession with *Frozen* as a warning? Mats liked the same things as always, but with greater intensity. Parallel to this, he developed a 'lecturing' manner, instead of wanting to converse and discuss.

After his diagnosis, another programme took over: *NCIS*. He could not get enough of these heroes. Episode after episode. But I realised that it gilded his daily life, which had become so drastically changed: medical appointments, medication, little to do, few social contacts, and the exertion of all his strength to heap love on me. I accepted that a series could lift his spirits and make him feel cheerful. Perhaps he enjoyed *NCIS* so much because he found his own history and dream. He recognised himself, the unconquerable man who had succeeded in (almost) everything he had made it his ambition to do. Except becoming a pilot. A defeat that he must have taken hard when it happened. Despite that, he did in fact become a pilot – a fighter pilot.

23 DECEMBER 2017

My flat is becoming my home. It feels nice, and yet it does not feel nice. At the same time as I delight in being able to see the sea and live in a beautiful place in an environment that suits me, I miss my life in the English countryside. This emptiness affects me almost every day. After such a long time abroad, moving home is a bit like moving to another country. Everything is always changing everywhere, not only places but we human beings too. English culture is part of me too, nowadays: the chatting with each other, and not just about the weather. One feels that people know one and that makes one happy – and the typical humour, the self-irony, are always there.

Coming back in the way I have done is difficult. Greater demands are made on me to settle down and to make something new out of my life. Grief has no natural place here – nothing here has any links to what happened, to the world of contacts of which I was a part. That was nothing I desired then, but something that I need now. Here, I have no connection with any healthcare team, or anyone who has seen and experienced the way he was those years, and how things were later towards the end. That is hard. I need to be in places that provide me with feedback on our fate, everything that belongs at home in England.

Mats would have liked our flat and I can see him lying on the sofa, just as he did towards the end of his life. He slept so much. Certainly fifteen hours a day. I never understood why, and said so often to his carers, and always received the same answer – it was the medicines. I believed that, because I no longer had the vitality to pursue an issue or to question anything.

The movements in his throat changed as his breathing deteriorated. But it was best that what happened, happened as it did, so that he and I and the children escaped the inevitable next level. He had a dignified end and we had something resembling contact that final morning. Then he was unconscious. I had never had to deal with death at close quarters. His tiredness was oxygen deficiency, and not just the medication. Carbon dioxide narcosis. On his death certificate, three causes are given: a, b and c, with a and b confirming the cause of respiratory failure and c including the names of both diagnoses.

24 DECEMBER 2017

When I decorated the Christmas tree with the children in 2017, I found a small piece of paper from January the same year, that I had put in the box with the Christmas balls. On it I had written that Mats was having a siesta at 14.30. I suppose I wrote it because I wondered where we would be in the whole process the coming Christmas.

And here we are now, in a flat in southern Sweden, with the children visiting, and us three trying to make a Christmas together. It feels unreal. We all feel rotten. Each of us needs to work through what Mats' illnesses have done to us during that time and afterwards. Almost everything has changed in these twelve months.

Four became three, England became Sweden for me, security and stability became anguish and anxiety, house became flat, a stimulating job became no job at all. Yet it is as though I have adapted and grown into this confused situation, bit by bit. I was probably forced to practise living with uncertainty and the oscillations of my existence by what happened. I was used to being alone, and have been helped by my independence. But this loneliness is different, new and now very definite.

I need to work through my grief. I was not at all prepared to feel as I do. Chaos and worry were the only constants from July to October, but that the end was near I did not anticipate. It hurts physically, it really hurts. What I brood over most of all is whether I gave my all. Did he feel alone, what did he think about, did he wonder if I would be there? My constant doubt creates anguish that is heavy to bear, and I am suffering from that. Imagine if we had been happy together those final years, on the marital level. Our memories, our children, our ups and downs. Phenomena like betrayal and closeness that existed side by side at the end. I had not done all I wanted to in my task of easing the way for him.

I dream that I am speaking for us both, and telling the stories of how deeply we fell in love, our wedding, when the children were born, travels, people we met and the adventures we had through moving abroad. I watch him smiling, laughing and gesticulating to show his feelings. Could I have made him any happier, more comfortable or more secure? Or was he happy perhaps, and even thankful deep inside that I was there for him the entire time? I must remind myself of our circumstances and be satisfied with not having given up, not having deserted him when our daily lives became worse and worse, more and more challenging. Small things became vital, is my conclusion.

29 DECEMBER 2017

'Fuck MND' became a catchphrase. Mats advocated for himself as well as he could, just as he had done with everything he had taken on or got involved in during his life. To his very last breath, he said he was going to be given treatment, in Sweden or in Switzerland. He was going to regain his health, even if I knew that that was not going to happen – no country had more to offer than any other country. Medically and scientifically, that is. But to know that he was convinced about this, that he trusted that something could be done for him – though not in England – there is something peaceful in knowing that, now, afterwards.

I noticed that he was aware of how thin and bony he had become. That changed his focus from August 2017 onwards. Suddenly he wanted to hurry up the medical procedure in which a PEG (Percutaneous Endoscopic Gastrostomy) feeding tube is placed directly through the abdominal wall into the stomach.

He wanted to gain weight. The trousers that I had bought for him in smaller sizes fitted him well. Yet he still wanted me to exchange them for a larger size. He wanted to have a size that was closer to his old physique. A size that matched what he still wanted to be. A number inside the trousers was evidence of what was happening to his body.

Difficulties in swallowing can also lead to imbalance in the metabolism. This metabolic disorder can cause the body to start breaking down the muscles to acquire energy, which can contribute to weight loss in people with ALS. (10)

How I have hated that hospital building and the ward signposted 'Neurology'. The reception, the waiting-room, and everything linked with the appointments to follow the course of the illness. If I felt like that, how did Mats feel about it? Perhaps he shielded himself, did not see himself as one of several patients who were there with the same diagnoses. Wheelchairs, breathing machines and relatives wiping saliva when their loved ones were no longer able to swallow. I do not believe that he thought: that's what it'll be like for me one day. I am fairly convinced of that.

My beloved husband, who had courted me with his romantic tactics all those years before. Did he love me deep in his heart, even when he behaved in completely the opposite way? When it came to the crunch, I was his choice. He regretted his actions. He was trapped by the thought that he might lose me. And he might have done. I was angry, unbelievably angry sometimes, desperately lonely in my thoughts about his having chosen to do what he did, without involving me – just bulldozing right over me. And now he himself was alone, and wanting to have me in his life more than anything else.

How thankful I am that my inner self guided me to be there through that torment, and to have a chance of living on with humility in the knowledge of how fragile life is. To have given the person I loved a worthy life, to have been his voice when he could no longer speak, his champion when he was no longer the strongest, his leader when he was vulnerable and his safeguard when he needed me most. This was the best I could do for the two of us, and for our children.

It took a couple of days after that crucial visit to the doctor on 19th September – when I realised his new situation for the first time – for me to decide that for my own best, not least, there was only one choice I could make: to stand by Mats' side with all my faith and resolution until he took his final breath. And so it was, and that will allow me and the children to find vitality and happiness again. Many memories will never be erased, but will only fade. And other memories will get stronger and stronger. Moments in a normal life, when we went hiking together, sat in the sun outside some pub or other, undertook a last journey, the whole family together. Also the everyday companionship around the kitchen table, when I ate, even though he could hardly eat anything any longer. How he enjoyed our being together; nothing else was of any importance.

31 DECEMBER 2017

My reaction the first time that I googled ALS is hard to think about. Here was a truth that perhaps might apply to our family. For a month after the diagnosis, I read more and more about the illness. Took it all in as well as I was able. Read about the stages, the course, figures and studies. The facts.

Then, however, something happened. I was on a hiking trip with some girlfriends, and the night before I left, Mats had lain there as so often, as close to me as he needed. I had felt how, now and then, his body suddenly jerked. Perhaps it was the illness, or perhaps it is something we all do in our sleep without being aware of it. But our first evening at our B&B, that memory popped up.

That night was the first of many when my arms and legs twitched uncontrollably, and I found it more and more difficult to fall asleep. Falling asleep and then waking up in the night became a pattern. It made me stop reading about the illness completely. I did not want to know any more. Knowing more did not make anything better. I talked to my psychologist about this and we focused on how I could break out of those recurring thoughts about the illness.

I feared going to bed – how alone and vulnerable I felt at night. And I could not wake him to be comforted, feel his warmth and understanding for my feelings. He was the one who was ill. His awareness of feelings had also faded – he was no longer able to read my face and interpret how I was feeling.

One technique that helped more than practical tools with figures and words in alphabetic order to break out of destructive thought patterns, was this: what more can happen to us human beings, what can we be exposed to and how can we cope with living with that? Then one mental image of life stuck out in my thoughts, about the many people who are living in war zones. How can they live with and deal with their terror in war? Not knowing anything about the next day, with no safety in their homes, perhaps not even having a home, not being able to protect their children and being in the midst of something in which one basically only has oneself and one's fear, at the mercy of chance for one's survival. Was it disrespectful, or immoral, to compare suffering that simultaneously gave a sense of perspective to our situation, so that fate acquired a slightly new dimension? This was about life and death too. Mats was going to die from ALS, but nobody knew when.

It helped a little to see how much people could cope with and how life is not fair, how one can end up in a reality that one cannot change however much one wants to. The panic attacks became fewer and not as frightening. We had some control and healthcare, of course, but no chance of a cure. However, there was the fundamental security that his physical need for help would always be met. All deterioration would be handled with qualified resources. And then we also had each other, our children and the people around us. This was nothing that he and I could talk about, and my way of reasoning would not have had any logic or value for him. With or without dementia, his only goal and focus was to be allowed to participate in a research project in which some new medicine offered hope of survival. A placebo group, the control group in all testing of new medicines, did not exist in his vision. He was going to get ahead.

2 JANUARY 2018

There were so many people who were thinking about us, wanting to help and doing so in every way they could think of. It is hard to stand to one side when one sees disaster strike somebody else. One feels helpless, despairing and probably wanting to do more than one is able. Perhaps it's difficult to know what to do, even to ask: 'How are things? How's it going? I feel so much for you.' People wanted to listen and share their reaction: 'I wish I could do something.' And that is all it takes. Some reassurance to know with certainty that one is not alone. I had (and have) all these wonderful people around me, who have shown me kindness and, in some way, walked by my side the whole time. They have been sympathetic and there for me. The same for Mats.

Now I know how little is in fact needed to help somebody in a crisis. To be allowed to talk, cry and express one's feelings in a single muddled outpouring when life is no longer what it has been. Nothing can change the situation, but human relationships can be decisive for how to handle living with it. Never stop making contact. One is so very alone anyway. Just say something – anything at all is better than silence and not being there.

3 JANUARY 2018

Recently I have been pondering in which order everything happened during the spring, and then in July, August and September 2016. By which I mean until 19 September. When did Mats realise that he was ill, not just stressed, but seriously ill? What made him give up his extra flat? Did he ask the doctors any questions? Did he only want to be with me again because he was ill? Or did his love affair come to an end? How long did their relationship last in reality? Probably longer than the months during which he had his own flat.

After a week on a language trip to France, in June 2016, I arrived home and interrogated him. There had been no point in ringing the day before, the day the disclosure was made. A normal dialogue by telephone was almost impossible in any case, and in this case, even more so. An e-mail in my daughter's inbox at her place of work. From the other woman's husband. In it, he revealed the relationship my husband had with his wife. We three, the children and I, had known nothing about it until that moment.

On 2 July 2016, we sat on a bench in our garden, Mats and I. I asked again and again what had happened. Who she was. I had also received that e-mail at my place of work, but I only discovered it on the Monday when I returned to work. There were many careless errors in one and the same message, that he sent to us both. Very badly adapted to fit both mother and daughter, since *'your father'* was sometimes sent to me and *'your husband'* was sometimes sent to her. Apart from that, the messages were identical:

> *Elizabet, the following message concerns your Husband Mats. I recommend you read this somewhere private as I assume most of what follows may be surprising and probably distressing.*

And the two-page-long email ends with:

> *You should know that I have sent a similar message to your daughter, I'm afraid I couldn't guarantee that this would reach you.*

It is so easy to find people nowadays. His ambition was to create aversion towards Mats from several directions. That probably made him feel better. He had spent a lot of time putting together two pages of text. A long story, the longest e-mail I have seen. She has turned this e-mail inside out, my darling daughter, and been angry, sad and pensive about the sender's conduct – how much satisfaction did he get out of it? A lot, I imagine. He hated Mats.

He did not succeed as well with me. I am not young, and that protected me somewhat. His words confirmed however what kind of person he himself was, and what he was capable of doing to harm us. Details about meetings, when it started, a trip to the sun that had been booked but cancelled. I wonder by the way which lie Mats would have used if it had happened, just going away then coming home suntanned in the middle of April and saying that he had been on holiday alone. Antigua.

In the text were many details about our family that are a sign of him and his wife having been in close contact, even if they were separated (which perhaps was the case). She must have told him about us. Was that the point at which they were considering a reunion, trying again, repairing their marriage? And why just then? Had Mats' health had any effect on the matter? Did the future look bleak with a lover who by then was almost unable to speak? Did Mats want her by his side, on visits to the doctors and the hospital? Did she want to be there in that case? Or was the adventure over now that uncertainties were knocking at the door? Or was it just over anyway? If it was over.

4 JANUARY 2018

The crux of my puzzle around this time was that Mats was not sad, not regretful, not moved; no tears and no scenes. He just admitted in the end, when he realised that I knew everything anyway. And he showed no signs of wanting to be with me instead, in July 2016. That came later, from nowhere, around the middle of August; that was when his tears came. Intensively and recurrently. Emotions just poured out of him. I have never seen my husband weep with such intensity, from deep inside, from the very heart of his being. I did not know how to relate to it. It was a total about-turn from ignorance to deep vulnerability and a profound need to be comforted.

How could I not try to comfort him – what was wrong, why was he crying now? He was in a void; he held his hands around my face and held it tightly and warmly. He kissed me on the lips, which he certainly knew that I did not want, a way of taking what he needed without my consent. My coldness at that moment is nothing I want to remember, but I could not find words and asked myself: what the hell is all this about, is this really my husband, what is wrong? What is happening, and what has happened to him?

As far as I know, there were no important appointments with the doctors those weeks, but on the other hand, one at the healthcare centre. It was the problem with phlegm that made him seek help there again. Since the antibiotics did not have any effect, he was finally referred to an ENT specialist.

Now things picked up speed, and the visit led to a referral to a neurologist, though not the same neurologist as had carried out his MRI scan six months earlier. The doctor had probably told him that he had a neurological illness, and that she was referring him to the hospital's specialists. But did she say what it was? I believe that she broached the subject, but that she held back because he did not have anyone with him – she wrote explicitly in her letter that she strongly recommended that he had his wife with him on the visit to the professor at the hospital on 19 September.

6 JANUARY 2018

Mats did not like Christmas or birthdays, despite being very traditional. He was a believer in his own way, but his faith was linked more to history and tradition than religion, as I experienced it. He was fascinated by astrology, and read about it daily. Even more since he fell ill, and that I can understand. However, the church and churchgoers reject astrology, do they not? Did he believe in the Christian god? Or was it another god? A person – a human being – who called himself God?

The astrologist from whom he bought information, or a divination, sent an uplifting message. Mats showed me these texts. Everything was going to get better. If he believed in this as a healthy person with plans for the future, he must have held onto it so much harder as an ill person. The doctors could not do anything to give him any hope of regaining his health. That was what he was seeking, something to hope for. Even if it had only been research, it would have given him hope.

He had also been in contact with somebody who called herself *Medium Spiritist*, followed by a Christian name. I saw this when he forwarded an e-mail to me that he had received from her. The subject of the message was: *The change that you are waiting for is on its way*. And then:

> *Mats,*
>
> *Yesterday evening one of my big meetings with my colleagues took an unexpected form. Because an unusual phenomenon occurred that concerned you directly. And we succeeded in doing something for you that nobody has succeeded with previously. This is going to free up the great changes that you're waiting for and open doors to a completely new life…A much happier life, I promise.*
>
> *Medium Spiritist (xxxxxx)*

What did he do with his thoughts all day? He was not working any longer, not meeting colleagues and friends to discuss and analyse things as he always had done before. History, politics, economy; what did he do instead, in his own world? He must have done a lot of thinking and been compelled to have contact with someone who gave him faith in the future and an urge to believe, and that was what the astrologist no doubt did, apart from anything else. And his very best friend of course.

My role was divided. First he turned his back on me and continued on his selfish track with riding, which seemed like his job, and with a woman who gave him kicks and had the power of attraction over him. Then, as if in a flash of lightning, I was everything, precisely everything. The person in his life who had his welfare in the palm of her hand.

Where then were all those others who had been so important in a social context that made him happy, in which he did not seem to miss me? I was not raised to that level, or interesting in the same way. Although when there was a risk that I might disappear and become just as focused on my own happiness as he was on his, that was when I became invaluable to him.

What am I supposed to do with all this? Feel loved? Feel cheated? I feel close to him, but ripped in two in my grief.

I struggled and I supported him, for his sake and for my sake. The alternative would have destroyed me then and now. Beloved Mats, you battled and never gave up. Convinced that you would be cured. Was it your faith, whatever that was – God or astrology – or did the dementia help you in some way to maintain a positive view of a hopeless fate? Or was it because you were the person you were, and never doubted your own power and capacity?

7 JANUARY 2018

Only two weeks or so after the diagnosis, Mats sought information intensively on research projects, and showed me what he had found in England: one project in Brighton and one in Sheffield. One of them focused on genetics. He became completely obsessed with both. He was going to participate. He told this to everyone.

As I write this, I feel how natural this search was. While we were in the midst of the shock of the diagnosis, and the destruction of a healthy life, I was unable to put myself in his place. I think I understood logically, but I can feel his trepidation more now when I no longer have him here with me. How was it possible to react in any other way? He was always so decisive and found ways to achieve whatever he wanted. So obviously he acted in exactly the same way with this.

When we had an appointment with the doctor shortly after the diagnosis, he wanted to discuss this. This time too there were medical students (or research students) with us in the room. That disturbed me, and I decided that I would ask for it to be changed for our next visit. I felt that it was degrading to have an audience learning from our tragedy. What the hell does it mean to them, compared with how it makes me feel? Do they sit there afterwards and say, 'It is quite usual that people become this desperate'?

Mats could hardly speak intelligibly even then. It cuts me like a knife thinking back on the comment from the doctor, when Mats had to get out his mobile and show what he had found since he was unable to express it: 'Please, can you put that away for now?' said the doctor, who was just then in the process of explaining something to us. How can anyone say a thing like that to somebody who is basically unable to speak, and who desperately wants to show something that he believes can help him to live instead of to die? Doctors and nurses know that there is no cure, and that nothing can be done to improve the diagnosis, so for them it is just the facts and their professional roles that decide their reactions and behaviour. But how is it for the patient? Can a doctor expect a patient to realise the situation immediately, to analyse the facts and accept the prognosis – that there is nothing at all to be done? I am going to die and must just wait for that, not knowing when, only how. Yet not exactly how, only that my body is going to lose its capacity to be mobile, and its ability to speak, swallow and breathe.

Bulbar paralysis is a form of ALS that starts in the muscles of the mouth, creating difficulties in swallowing and indistinct speech. The word 'bulbar' refers to the part of the cerebral cortex where the damaged nerves are found, the corticobulbar region. Many patients with bulbar ALS are unable to speak or eat, but can walk and write. Patients with bulbar ALS usually have a more rapid course of illness than those patients who first notice symptoms in arms or legs. These patients usually develop bulbar symptoms as the illness progresses. (11)

Working in a field like ALS demands active engagement in research, and perhaps being able to participate in solving the riddle one day. Just as Mats had always had a passion for his professional work, so it shifted to being a passion to work for a solution to survive ALS. How was he supposed to take in logical arguments, facts, and think that it was just as well to let go, give up, stop searching for solutions, since the doctors said that it was incurable? Even so, there is still so much to do in this field before there is a cure, or a truly effective medication to slow down the course of the illness.

8 JANUARY 2018

What could one do that was not done for Mats? Between medical facts and *nothing*, there is something. Ask the patients what would be meaningful? Ask those closest to them? What kind of response would there be? Medical support is given priority and it is important to have routines for that. However, the psychological and mental sides are almost ignored and not taken seriously enough, in my experience. The waiting list for an appointment with a psychologist in the MND team was far too long, also in our case. It should have been an unquestionable right for everyone in the family. The possibility does exist, but yet it does not, since it is only for a costly sum if the need is acute. A meeting should be offered immediately. At any rate if there is to be the extra value of meeting a psychologist knowledgeable in neurology and the implications of the trauma of a diagnosis like ALS.

So the patient could be dead before this support is given without cost, as I learned from my psychologist. I was lucky that I was able to pay, because I was called to my first and only appointment without charge after Mats had died. It was actually offered to me at the end of September, that is, two weeks before the day of his death. But then there was no longer any point in talking – my only focus was to get life to function every hour. One hour at a time. One hour at a time. That was why I cancelled. What my psychologist had said was basically also true in my case.

Are there the same deficiencies when it comes to other illnesses? Serious illnesses but with a survival prognosis? There are fields in which enormous steps forward have been taken, just as things should be. I burn for the same thing to be the case for those who have been afflicted by ALS, and their families. Why is that not the case already? Because that illness is so rare? It can surely not possibly be because it is expensive? It cannot be operated on or cured by medication. Therefore I must ask: how common is it that one takes up a bed in a hospital or a home for longer periods while the illness is being managed?

9 JANUARY 2018

Was it dementia that drove him to live life differently? Helping himself to what he wanted without taking responsibility for his behaviour? I know now, afterwards, that the woman he preferred may have been meaningful to him for a long time before I got to know of her. As early as the summer or autumn of 2014, after that wedding that we had all attended. The unfaithfulness in itself was not dementia. There are many who are unfaithful, and these people do not all have dementia, do they? Nor does she.

Obviously she wanted to get a divorce from her husband, though they had two small children. What were Mats' and her future plans, apart from a dream holiday in April 2016? The one that could have taken place behind my back, but that Mats had to give up when something else interfered with their plans. Did she go? I happened to find the transaction in our bank statement, since the hotel had been paid for far in advance. Was this a life together that was first to be tested a little? Or an opportunity for an adventure that neither of them could resist?

When I think back on the years before the diagnosis, I see odd actions that did not stand out so much then as now when I know. He chose lies instead of honesty and dialogue. What made him believe that I would try to stop him from choosing a new life? Perhaps he did not want to have that all the time? But the months that he lived for the moment gave me time to reflect and contemplate.

When did he fall ill? That question is one I often come back to. FTD certainly came first. That was the professor's opinion, and that seems to be correct now that we know. If we look back, we can see the pieces falling into place. A stranger and stranger conduct, a kind of anger that lacked relevance. He slapped himself more and more often in the face with the palm of his hand – first one side, then, as if he were turning the other cheek, the other. Lack of awareness of when he was boring the people around him with a subject that he had got stuck in and refused to let go of. He could not change his track, but almost forced people to listen. This disturbing and sometimes antisocial behaviour must have been the onset of dementia.

10 JANUARY 2018

The fact that he so often said that he loved me – was that truly what he felt or was it regret for what he had done? Did he wonder what might happen, and grasp desperately after a way to keep me in his life, by overwhelming me with love? I said often that I had never considered abandoning him, that I would always be there by his side and help him. At the same time, I had to be honest and say what I felt inside myself, that he had taken away my trust in him and thereby also in us; that I no longer wanted to be in the background, or overshadowed by his values. Most of all I did not want to be overshadowed by his passion for people who were not like me. It was not about not being able to forgive, it was about balance and faith being exhausted and gone. My integrity and respect for myself had to come first now. My commitment to feeling well, listening to myself and living in another way. But being there, in the midst of the hell in which we found ourselves, was something I had no doubts about at all.

One evening when we were sitting on the sofa, shortly after the diagnosis, he looked terribly sad. I said so, and asked what he was thinking about most. 'That I betrayed you', he said. 'I forgive you', I said. 'Thank you', came his response. These words mean everything to me. That was a pivotal moment. Think, that we were able to talk to each other like that despite everything. He was of course much sicker than I realised then, since the FTD diagnosis had not yet been made. That came a few weeks later.

I slept badly and was emotionally exhausted. I was often sad, and crying was a release but also tiring. Mats was unable to read my feelings. When I said that I had slept badly, he replied: 'Why on earth?' I could really see in his eyes that he did not understand. Later, it was explained to me that the illnesses affect the ability to read facial expression and to feel empathy. This was clearly what was happening, making him unable to draw the conclusion that his illness had an impact on me that made me anxious, sad and upset.

11 JANUARY 2018

When the children went back to England after Christmas, it felt incredibly empty. I made up things that I felt I had to do to keep busy, and dispel my thoughts. It was impossible to grasp what had happened.

Shocking, and with no forewarning. How fast and suddenly it had all happened. Before my eyes, everything fell to bits in just a few weeks, barely four to be exact. I wonder what he thought, if he thought, and whether he experienced my presence the day he died. I cannot stop thinking about his suffering and am set on finding answers. Was the illness continually in his thoughts? How did he handle the situation in his mentally distorted world? Perhaps the illnesses had been in his body for many years, while we were blissfully unaware.

I have saved all the letters sent by the doctors to Mats. All the letters that he probably would have thrown away otherwise. I am thankful for that now, because it is a part of my grieving process to go over and over everything that happened and try to understand at a deeper level when he should have begun to fear the gravity of the letters' contents. Now I read and pieced things together, and it tied me in knots when I turned over one letter where he had written on the back: 'please, forgive me!' It was written in red and must have been meant for me. That was when he was back with me again, in our home, when his 'holiday home' had played out its part. Had the other woman also played out her part?

He was completely overjoyed to be with me and could not demonstrate it enough. Did he tell her that he was ill, and how ill he was? What did she feel if she knew? In some way, they kept in contact, she and Mats, and also her husband. That was made clear in the summer of 2017 in July when Mats committed a crime. Who took the initiative to keep up the contact? Mats could no longer speak and barely write either. Something tells me that there was no interest in just cutting him off. In that case she would have changed her e-mail address and mobile phone number, would she not?

13 JANUARY 2018

For a while, I believed that I would be receiving a telephone call or a letter from the healthcare centre, after Mats had died. But nobody rang and nobody wrote. Was that handled correctly? Actually, I had not heard much during the period of his illness either, apart from the fire-arms issue. A letter did arrive on another occasion too, it is true. In it he was asked to contact the healthcare centre to book an appointment for a blood test. That was in the midst of it all – neither at the beginning nor the end.

If one is taking Riluzole, which can injure the liver, one's blood is checked regularly. Since Mats did not reply on our home telephone or his mobile, they sent him a letter. I was not at home on that occasion, and therefore nobody had answered the telephone. He had stopped answering a long time before, since he was unable to speak. In the letter, he was asked to make contact, to ring or write, so that they could update his contact information. I suppose they thought that something had been changed, since he did not answer. Instead of reading his journal where they could see that he had ALS/FTD, and might have suspected that he did not reply because he could not. Since he could not speak.

That letter made me both sad and angry. Mostly because I wondered where their support was in everything we were going through. When it came to a routine like a blood test, they made contact, but it seemed as though they had no idea which illnesses he had. I wrote a letter and told them how upset I felt. A while afterwards, I received a phone call from the healthcare centre's practice manager. We had a good conversation and she radiated warmth. At last, I thought, at last they understand that we are here and are really in need of involvement from their side. I thought therefore that everything would be better, that the communication that was needed between us had now been initiated. But nothing changed.

Imagine if the lack of contact, that I made clear by criticising the healthcare centre, had shaken up the routines. How would our life have looked from spring/summer until October 2017 if a care plan had been initiated from December 2016? From the day that we knew with certainty that Mats was suffering from an additional neurological illness. Nine months of medical knowledge had been entirely wasted.

15 JANUARY 2018

My mood shifts, just as expected. Two things have helped me a lot the past weeks. The meeting with the professor in the company of my daughter, a couple of weeks after the funeral, to understand what caused death to come so suddenly and unexpectedly. But now I know that deterioration in ALS can happen drastically. I also think of the extra day for which I have the carer, who was on duty that morning, and the ambulance men, to thank. And I want to have it back. And the day before. And the day before that. When it happened, I still did not believe that we were at the end. I believed that we would soon be living in Sweden, the two of us – and that his life would end here.

How do we human beings function in acute situations? One does things, but does not have time to think or reflect. If I look at that day from the outside, it was without any doubt the end – yet, those hours given to us by the actions of the carer and the emergency services meant that the children could say farewell to their father. There was sufficient time for them to get out to the hospital and be with us in pain and love. The whole family. The circumstances that made that possible I can only describe as *a wonder*.

It was not possible for me to be at home and watch over everything around the clock. Ordinary life and our home were there, and they were my responsibility. If I had been out shopping for food in the morning that day then Mats would have passed away all alone. According to the doctor, it would have been peaceful, but for me it would have been a catastrophe and a burden to bear. To have been there all the way but not be there then. Despite the horrors of that abominable emergency department, where we were, all four of us - the memory of it is not at all terrible. On the contrary, it is a memory that helps us in our grief more than anything else.

My need is palpable, to talk and think things through to the end, concerning that last period, and all we went through. Longterm acceptance, that I did what I could. My human limits that meant that an unpleasant side of me sometimes appeared when nothing else produced results. Frustration, uncertainty, demands and stress in a daily life that may be compared to a roller coaster. One reaches a level that one thinks one can cope with, then one is at the bottom again. In that there is now an insight into what one can handle and control, although the journey is jerky and demanding.

There were days when I wanted to flee from everything, race away, pack my bag and hand over the responsibility to somebody else. I wanted to hide myself somewhere where nobody could find me. Become normal again. But I never actually approached the point when I might have done that. Only in my thoughts, because I knew that I belonged at home with Mats every day and every night. To be his voice and a guarantee for as tolerable a life as possible.

Sometimes I am overpowered by strong feelings of guilt and anguish, because I wish I could have done things much better. That will pass if I listen to myself. I gave him everything, absolutely everything that I was able to give

in our complicated circumstances. Can I ever
be sure that things were as good as they could
possibly be?

16 JANUARY 2018

One of Mats' many interests was hunting. His weapons were not always locked away in a weapon cabinet. His licence had been renewed according to all the rules and laws throughout the years abroad, and of course the police in England had all relevant information about everything. One day in April 2017, the police arrived at our house when I was not at home.

A month or so earlier, I had organised for the guns to be locked up in the weapon cabinet at the home of good friends in the village. It had worried me for a while to see firearms in our wardrobe, as though they were tennis racquets or golf clubs. Particularly since the diagnosis of dementia had been made.

The only occasion that I received a spontaneous phone call from our GP was at the beginning of 2017. She started off by asking how we were doing and how I was coping with the situation. I thought for a second that that was what she rang for and appreciated her concern. But then she asked the real question: there were weapons registered in Mats' name at our address and she wondered where he kept them? 'The guns are locked up according to the regulations,' I said. Quick thinking, the solution would have to come later. My theory was this, that when a diagnosis of dementia is made, the information is checked against the police register, and that was the way healthcare came to know that a firearms licence existed. But was the opposite true – that the register on firearms licences took account of diagnoses on dementia? That would be logical from the point of view of risks. The healthcare centre to which we belonged during the period of illness had obvious shortcomings. It was far too big and lacked the quality of our previous healthcare centre linked to our former address. Our new one had an extensive catchment area that was probably more demanding. I often wondered why we never received a visit or a telephone call after the serious diagnosis had been made. All the letters from specialists always go to the patient's GP at the healthcare centre to which one belongs, so the information was available there. Only one letter arrived, with the confirmation of information about the ALS diagnosis, in which the doctor who had signed it also said how sorry she was. Then nothing more. Nothing at all after the diagnosis of dementia.

The guns must be locked up, and I wanted to do that without discussion. I did not know how Mats would react to that. Say yes or no, or 'no way' as he had begun to say more and more. It actually got slightly comical. When he was resting, I carried first one weapon and then the other downstairs, in their heavy leather cases. I was nervous that he would wake up. I had to be quick. Step one done, everything was there in the hall, well hidden. After that, I went out to the boot of my car. I had an arrangement with friends in the village, who fetched and locked up the weapons in their weapon cabinet. What a relief.

I was careful to have everything ready before our trip to the Canary Islands. A trip we undertook all four of us, and that we were longing to do. Good thing the weapons were taken care of beforehand. One week or so before we were due to leave, I noticed that Mats was searching for something in the wardrobe, and he found what he was looking for – a gun. Imagine if we had had a surveillance camera in the bedroom – a picture of my face then would have been really worth seeing.

There he was, standing with the gun in his hands and inspecting the sights, and I shouted loudly: 'put that away' and wondered at the next moment how the hell it had got there? The cases were locked up, but one of them was empty. The gun had stood leaning against the wall of the wardrobe, behind a suit. I had not even noticed the difference in weight when I had carried the cases to my car. What a farce – but he agreed later to that gun also being locked up, since we were going to be away on holiday. A good argument that he accepted. I would probably have been able to persuade him anyway, really, seeing how it turned out, but I did not want to take the risk that he might become aggressive and unwilling. Saving energy and avoiding unnecessary conflicts – that became a way of thinking and living.

17 JANUARY 2018

Mats thus received a spontaneous visit from the police. I am guessing that they rang the doorbell and then just walked in and explained that they wanted to see his firearms licence. I wonder what he did. Did he hunt for it or the guns? How could he tell them anything? It must have been impossible for the police to understand him. How did they react? An authoritative attitude, arrogance, kindness? Afterwards, I thought that it was a good thing I was not at home.

Somehow they had got hold of the number to my mobile and they rang me up the same day when I was on my way home from work. A man with power wanted to know a number of things. I wondered if it really was right just to walk into our home without giving any notice? 'Oh yes we can,' he said. Of course, but it was the way that he said it. At that point I exploded, which happened sometimes, and asked if he had any idea what was wrong with my husband's speech. 'It was a bit difficult to make sense of things,' he said. Then when he had to listen to my views on how they could have proceeded, his attitude suddenly changed and his tone became more human: 'I completely understand what you are going through.' 'Do you?' I thought then.

I shall never get to know the whole story, but it had nothing to do with any cross-referencing of registers. At least, I want to hope that if that had been the case, then they would not have proceeded in that way. Then they would have cooperated more suitably with the health-care centre and me, and resolved the matter with respect, of course with certain haste, and planned the visit together with us.

Mats ought definitely not to have a fire-arms licence any longer. It appeared soon that the licence had in fact expired. That was what had given the signal to the police and led to the circus with the home visit. He had applied for a new licence, although I had begged him not to, because I wanted to spare him the humiliation of a refusal. It was not completed since neither the form nor the cheque was correctly filled in. I believe that he forgot the whole matter shortly afterwards.

18 JANUARY 2018

When the second diagnosis came it was in many ways a relief. The children and I slowly took in why he had been behaving so oddly for quite a long time. There was even a comment in an email that I had written, in which I explained the event concerning Arlanda and finished the sentence with the words: 'it is almost as though he has dementia.' He had rung from Arlanda, as always when he had been out travelling and was on his way home. He rang me nearly every day.

He rang me to tell me that something had happened at the airport. He was going to be late or unable to come home at all. I asked what had happened, but he could not tell me in a normal, structured way. I think there was a blizzard, but all he said was mixed up with such anger and frustration that nothing sensible came out. Everything was just hellish; he was angry and unable to focus on what he wanted to say. Now this is one of the many pieces of the jigsaw showing how the frontotemporal dementia had started to come creeping in.

I want to understand as much as possible about in which order the changes occurred. Understand when and how they started. My son reminded me of an awful incident, when his schoolfriends turned up spontaneously at our home one day. A completely normal occurrence in any home at all with young people living at home. Mats rushed out of our house and yelled at them, partly in German. Nothing had happened, they just turned up in a car and parked in the drive. But he told them to go to hell, gesticulating wildly with his arms.

I suffer with my son when I see this scene before me. A sensitive age with 'normal' parents for whom one is often embarrassed anyway – how did he feel standing there and seeing his dad behaving like a madman? Crazy behaviour. Those poor chaps never wanted to set foot at our place again.

I told him what I thought about it, how terribly he had behaved. I do not remember his response in detail, but he would never admit that he had done something wrong. I think he struck himself on the forehead as he so often did, and said something to the effect of our son's friends being rubbish. How can one judge one's children for being uncertain teenagers? How can one judge their friends, whom one does not always know very well during their teenage period? During that period in their lives, parents are rather uninteresting. Something must have been damaged in his brain as early as that; his filter, his tact for how to behave and speak to others. His reaction was definitely not normal. That was in 2014.

19 JANUARY 2018

The lack of empathy for situations with which he did not agree is another example. I had been working for several years in England, in the field in which I had experience: education. After some years at a school, I wanted to develop my career and aim for a post at the university. I never received any support, just criticism that I was going about things in totally the wrong way: 'Bugger all the adverts, just go straight in and sell yourself.' That is what he said, without acquiring any deeper knowledge of my field of work. It was the opposite of his: public and traditional with rigid patterns to be matched, not the same new thinking as in his field of business. He spent no time in listening or exchanging ideas and possibilities. It was upsetting.

That side of him asserted itself more and more. When I eventually succeeded and received a good offer to work with administration at the university, he showed no happiness that I was feeling happy. He showed no pride that I had attained my goal. He did not even know which college I was working for. For him, I was working at the university and that was enough information. He wished me well, but was not interested in what motivated me. I do not know why that was so, but other people's ambitions seemed more important, grander. If one shared his focus and ambitions, one acquired his focus, was the conclusion I came to. In any case in our private life. Was this the illness starting to have effect, or was it quite simply his personality that manifested itself more strongly later in life?

I admire him for several things that he did in his life, the things he succeeded in doing. All the goals he had declared openly and then achieved. I know that he was an outstandingly good person to work with. Direct, clear, fair and with great trust in others' capacity. And not at all interested in micro-management; he wanted to give people freedom and allow them to grow. Without any tendency to be threatened by their competence and driving force. He liked it, and highlighted it. A product of many years in the defence forces perhaps? 'The best leadership education,' he called it. Working with him must have been developmental – with space for independence and personal responsibility. However, that side of him was not present at home in the same way.

20 JANUARY 2018

On 1 December 2016, the diagnosis fronto-temporal dementia was established. We were both interviewed by a clinical psychologist, in a room with a view over the cemetery close by. Did the psychologist not find this view uncomfortable, given the circumstances and prognosis of what he was assessing? Mats was thereafter assessed with the help of further tests, almost exclusively on a computer, I believe. I had to wait in the office while this took place.

He had with him the book we were given when he received his ALS diagnosis two and a half months earlier, I do not know why. But the report mentions that he had the book with him, and I wonder whether that was considered odd. He was cheerful when we were there. There was an assistant to the psychologist who knew a little Swedish; I think her mother was Swedish. We talked about that, and that we were from Sweden, and it was probably a way to lighten the mood a little. However, I do not think that Mats grasped what was to be tested or investigated that day.

This is an unusual form of dementia that expresses itself in a completely different way from other dementia illnesses. Dementia with symptoms from the frontotemporal lobes has its onset early on in the typical cases, sometimes before the age of 50. The memory and thought capacity are often well preserved in frontotemporal dementia, while changes in personality can be noticed early on in the illness, with decreased capacity for judgement. The person may stop bothering about personal hygiene for example, and the emotional life is blunted. The person often becomes easily irritated. The ill person does not her or himself experience any great changes in personality.

The memory is often only affected towards the end in frontotemporal dementia. The front parts of the brain regulate among other things our personality and much of the social

behaviour and the self-control that are needed
for us to function. Capacities like concentration, planning, insight and judgement are
steered from there, as are impulse control and
aggressivity. Even the capacity to express ourselves, our speech, is controlled by the frontotemporal lobes. In frontotemporal dementia,
the nerve cells atrophy and die in the frontal sections of the brain. The actions and the
thoughts that are controlled by this part of the
brain deteriorate in function. When the nerve
cells in the brain's frontal regions atrophy, the
connections are also broken between the nerve
cells that link the various sections of the frontotemporal lobes together with each other and
other parts of the brain. In frontotemporal
dementia, the personality is often affected first.
A person may seem reserved, have difficulty
in getting involved and have difficulties in following customs and etiquette. Concentration
difficulties are also common. Sometimes a person is also affected by mental symptoms like
depression and apathy.

- *Frontotemporal dementia is relatively unusual*
- *Onset in typical cases is early on, sometimes before the age of 50*
- *Personality changes are noticeable early on in the illness*

Further on in the illness, the person afflicted becomes more tired and apathetic. Speech deteriorates and the person has difficulties in remembering. In severe illness, the person is totally without insight, most often without speech and unable to interpret the surroundings and bodily signals; however, the person can usually function relatively well physically. What exactly triggers the illness and causes the deterioration of the nerves is not known. However, researchers have in a number of cases found a hereditary disturbance that can be linked to the illness. Frontotemporal dementia is relatively unusual. Of the people suffering from dementia illnesses in Sweden, about 7,500 are estimated to have frontotem-

poral dementia. There is no difference between the sexes. (12)

In Mats' case, frontotemporal dementia was established, using among others sentences like the following:

In summary I do not think he has the mental capacity to consent to clinical trial and there is clear evidence of significant cognitive and behavioural change consistent with behavioural variant FTD [...]. He had a strong misunderstanding that being enrolled in the trial would somehow change his motor neurone disease by improving his immune system and allowing a normal life span. Behaviourally he did appear disinhibited but not grossly so [...].

21 JANUARY 2018

The day after came the telephone call from the psychologist, in which he confirmed the suspicion that the professor had had. Mats had frontotemporal dementia. I know that I was sitting at my writing desk at college when I received the message, and it was as though one thing after another just got worse. It was unreal, yet expected. I asked for a meeting with him, because it was far too inadequate just to talk like that on the phone. I would be given an appointment.

Which other illnesses are diagnosed without any measure taken afterwards? Does that happen in cases of purely physical illness? Diabetes, asthma, rheumatism and goitre, for example? Yet frontotemporal dementia is a physical illness too, but with mental and psychological symptoms, being an illness that affects the brain.

It is true that it is incurable and cannot be treated with medicines, but why was nothing done to build up a contact network for the person who was next of kin and taking care of the sufferer? This person was living with the patient every day and becoming responsible for more and more. Would it be my fault if he damaged anything? Imagine if he injured somebody, by unawareness or lack of judgement – who would be to blame? Who would take the consequences if that happened? And how would I be able to live with and carry that on my shoulders? What would it have cost, in terms of time and medical resources, to arrange for me to know where to turn when things got too difficult?

It would have provided security and something to hold onto when the situation became acute. Like the time when Mats disappeared. He was not at home when I arrived back from work and did not respond when I texted him. He was a person who held his mobile in an iron grip from the moment he woke up. The car was not there. At that point I was going crazy – he had disappeared without a trace, which he had never done before. I sent emails to many friends and to some people in healthcare as well, because

I was desperate to know his whereabouts. For his safety, and that of others too.

Everybody responded thank goodness, but nobody knew where he was, only that he was not with any of them. Late in the evening, he arrived back home and could not explain where he had been. 'Where have you been?' 'Nothing', he replied. 'Nothing' was all I ever got to know – as he wrote on a piece of paper. When this occurred, we were approaching the storm, the urinary tract infection that he contracted one month before his body gave up.

22 JANUARY 2018

Why was there no plan of action for when the dementia became frighteningly apparent, and it was impossible for me to cope with everything on my own? One of the doctors' letters stated clearly that the illnesses would be a challenge for us:

'Both Mr and Mrs ... are facing one of the most challenging situations with the worst aspects of two difficult neurodegenerative disorders.' In another letter it was further stated: *'... it has become very clear that there is significant behavioural impairment as part of his FTD, with loss of insight and concerns over lack of judgement.'*

When frontotemporal dementia has been established, when the aggressive course of the illness is known, and that it is even more aggressive in combination with ALS, and when there is no doubt about the diagnosis being true, then what more is there to know before help is planned or offered? What were they waiting for? Nothing was done in good time to make preparations to deal with the frontotemporal dementia.

ALS continued to be the main focus, and it was followed up, and measures were taken as and when various functions deteriorated: control over breathing, ensuring nutrition via a PEG, monitoring weight loss, medication with Riluzole and expectorants. Particularly important and a must. Here we were completely covered by a system that accompanied us to the end. I had a list of telephone numbers I could ring at any time. A well-structured safety net to cover everything for which there was no cure or improvement. However, frontotemporal dementia just kind of existed there, accepted and described in a long, detailed report, a confirmation of the course of the illness – and then nothing more.

If it was a matter of logistics, surely the solution was simple? Two departments, specialist clinics in the healthcare system should have linked up with each other to provide the best possible help for the whole family. Just as the established routine was that the healthcare centre's doctor should be in contact during the whole period of illness. A continual exchange of information with the specialist responsible for details – neurologist in this case – while the GP at the healthcare centre had the overall responsibility for the patient's total care needs. The total picture. That was what was missing and I cannot understand why.

23 JANUARY 2018

Many must have noticed how Mats changed from 2015 onwards, or in any case from 2016. I heard of course how he spoke in a different way with more effort with clients and colleagues. He worked from home on certain days, and his mobile rang constantly. And even the woman he was already meeting at that time must have noticed the change in his speech. Did anyone say anything to him at any point? Or was that too sensitive? One has not got the right to interfere, and one does not want to risk insulting anybody.

When I myself confronted him on the subject in the spring of 2015, he said at once that yes, he was finding it difficult sometimes to get hold of words. His opinion was that a business situation had affected him for a time and created great pressure. When he was not blaming stress, his attitude was that it was his voice that was the cause. He never said that it was his speech that was the problem, just that his voice was crap. That was a word he used often.

UNTIL WE KNEW, TWICE: LIFE WITH MND/ALS AND FTD

In my thoughts I assume that he made a dis-
tinction between speech and voice, in which
speech is linked to the brain while voice is
linked to the throat. Therefore the cause of
the symptoms might be an infection, instead
of damage to the brain. It must have been both
worrying and frightening not to have full control over his speech. Not to recognise himself
– his status turned upside down. He also had
to take more of a backseat in groups since he
was unable to take any initiatives by means of
language, which had been his trademark, dom-
inating discussions.

This became obvious one day when a fine
card arrived from a colleague, in February 2017.
An utterly fantastic card, with a message that
he wanted to visit us, he really wanted to meet
Mats. Genuine consideration, and it was partly
because he had encountered the illness before
in his own family. When I read the card, I said
straight away that we must invite him home
for a coffee. 'No way', was the response, and I
did not at first understand why. Then I realised
that Mats now saw himself as less impressive,

quieter and possibly weaker. He wanted to be seen as the person he really was. Was my conclusion correct? I ignored his reaction in any case, partly because I wanted to take this outstretched hand, and partly because it was not a good thing to isolate ourselves from our surroundings. I contacted him and invited him to our home.

When the day arrived and he came in through the door, Mats was incredibly cheerful. We sat at the kitchen table, the three of us, talking and drinking coffee. There was not much he was able to say with words, but with pen and paper and a helping heart from his colleague, much was said despite everything. Thank heavens I was starting to be more dominant, taking decisions like this one. Meetings like this, personal meetings face to face, were the best, because then he did not disappear into a role in which he was alone and unhappy. In groups, he became more the kind of person he actually was not, but had once been.

There is another important memory of a social context. A family came to visit us, a friend of Mats' whom I had contacted after the diagnosis, because I was uncertain whether he knew or not. He did not, but since that day he kept in frequent contact with us both. That family was coming to England on holiday for a week that summer, and I invited them to our home for lunch. Mats was completely okay with that.

The sun was shining and we sat out in the garden. It was not easy to see him being left out, as I experienced it, but I do not think that he himself felt it that day. It was in June. He was able to eat a little, but it took him a long time. He was cheerful and laughed, and we did all we could to include him in the discussions. After eating, Mats took a walk in the village with his faithful friend and the friend's family. That was a gorgeous day.

24 JANUARY 2018

Considering the initial symptoms of ALS, and how it can resemble certain other illnesses, it is essential to get a second neurological opinion. A vast majority of those diagnosed with ALS have what is regarded as 'sporadic' ALS. Then there is no explanation for the onset of the illness, meaning that the cause or causes of the disease are unknown.

There is a contact between ALS doctors that is probably special, since the illness is so uncommon. Everyone seems to know everyone. Mats was brilliant at finding the right person and he wanted a second opinion in some other country than England.

That came about, and he was optimistic and expectant when he left for Switzerland, ten weeks after his diagnosis. The ALS diagnosis. When he came back, he was positive and told me that now he would be getting help, and that he would first and foremost be included in their research. When the letter with the test results came, it showed exactly the same description and diagnosis as had been confirmed in England. *'ALS with bulbar onset… some executive concerns.'*

However, for him it was still not like that. He had not filtered the contents, but believed instead sincerely in a possibility. This was not because he had met a doctor who was not serious, on the contrary, he was a completely fantastic professor. It was how he had been received, the way in which they had talked to him – I accompanied him there six months later. The atmosphere was different. They truly listened to what Mats himself desperately wanted to say, that he had read about quinine among other things. Even though he could barely make himself understood, they made sure he was given a hearing. They wholeheartedly made him the centre of their attention, and the doctor steered Mats' jerky concentration throughout the conversation with calm empathy and respect, while explaining the facts. Several times, once more, pausing, starting again, pausing, starting again, while he explained that quinine had no effect whatsoever on ALS.

I enjoyed being allowed to experience this, and it was the kind of evidence that I needed then, that one can do *nothing* in so many different ways. Mats accepted his words and slowly took in the message and never mentioned quinine again. That was in April 2017, and we left with a prescription for Riluzole with which he seemed satisfied. After that we needed to find a pharmacy as fast as ever we could. Could it be the case that he had realised that medical research was ruled out? Otherwise he would probably not have wanted to start taking medication, would he? Or had his faith and other resources started to dry up – did the dementia influence the will and strength he had shown up until then?

25 JANUARY 2018

In February 2017 we travelled to La Gomera. It was wonderful to be together all four of us, without a single hospital appointment – away from the winter and our home and to the sun. It was something that the clinical psychologist had mentioned to me, and suggested when I visited him after the dementia diagnosis. That we could create new, fresh memories and enjoy everything that we were still able to do. I am so happy that it actually happened.

Since the children were small, we have been on many trips – in Sweden, Belgium, England and from there to other places. They took place over a period of about twenty years when the children were growing up; fond and important memories. We were stubborn in our choice to stay at B&Bs, charming and special, of which there are plenty in England. The children complained sometimes, and said that we were boring since we did not book large hotels with swimming pools and other luxuries. We shared that, the two of us, choosing the more natural, simple and personal environments.

I had prepared the journey itself very carefully and done everything to avoid stress. Checking in was a process that Mats had never taken calmly. He should *never* need to wait! The travel agent had therefore booked special assistance. Gatwick was chaos, jam-packed with people who were leaving for the February holiday. A week I would normally avoid, but for various reasons we were compelled to choose it.

Just seeing the swarms of people and long queues to every desk made Mats start waving his arms around. I went up to one employee and showed our documents, and she took us to a desk where we were allowed to go to the front of the queue. The looks from all the other people were not kind. 'Who the hell do you think you are,' I could almost hear them saying. 'You wouldn't want to change places with us, believe me,' I thought then. No wheelchair, no crutches, and no bandages were to be seen and nobody was elderly, so the only remaining explanation was cheating if one was allowed to go first in the queue.

Then came the security check. There we were going to be allowed to use the fast track – however, the staff there assumed we had taken the wrong track and pointed out where we should be instead. Perhaps I could not blame them, but anger was seldom far off at that time: it was my friend and my weapon. I produced the evidence and then we were allowed to proceed. The exact same procedures took place when we flew home a week later.

26 JANUARY 2018

On holiday it was often obvious just how ill Mats was, because he said strange things, made weird signs with his hands and was generally odd, far from the norm. We suffered with him and were also ashamed of him at the same time. I saw in their ways of looking at us that certain people dissociated themselves. His speech was almost gone, and he had to clap his hands to get attention from the waiters. What else was he supposed to do? It was not at all strange, but could be interpreted as treating people like servants. Politeness has no place in that kind of language and dialogue, somehow.

His loss of weight was now beginning to show and his body was thinner, though his face was still well-rounded with healthy features and a gorgeous tan. The day we were due to return home, I sat in a deckchair lapping up the last of the summer warmth and observing him at the same time as he walked around near the pool. It looked as though he was thinking and reflecting – just think of all the times we have been on holiday when he radiated a zest for life, happiness and confidence, tested sports and took every opportunity to dive. Times when he had used his body as he wanted, as it pleased him.

That man had partly disappeared, and this man was of another kind. There was suddenly a lump in my throat then, because I realised that this was in all probability his and our last holiday trip. The clarity of the thought that, yes, well, he is not going to be as healthy as he is now for very much longer. I wondered what he was philosophising about while he was walking around there, round and round, without sitting down.

It is hard to think about that moment. Will that pain ever be erased? That moment in time is like a film in my inner eye. Sometimes I enjoy it, but sometimes I want to destroy it. It is one of the hundreds of times when I felt so unbelievably, infinitely sorry for him. How unfair to have to ascertain that he was just continuing on the downward path to getting worse and worse. Bloody, hellish ALS. To see without being able to change anything, without being able to take it away. All I could do was to help him, remain with him, and give him more love. Did he need even more love than the love he received?

That week has been invaluable to me. Having a few newer and finer memories to look at is a gift in the midst of this grief. Knowing how he enjoyed the sun, good food and a good appetite, without any greater problems in swallowing. It is these small moments that soothe among the images of more difficult moments. It always hurts to think about ALS, and it would be a lie to say anything else. It is such a relentless, hopeless, utterly cruel disease.

27 JANUARY 2018

I will never have all the facts about why he van-
dalised a car. It was the soft-top foldable roof
of an Audi that he totally destroyed in a car-
park with about 700 parking spaces. Mats was
caught red-handed. What was he doing there
at that outlet that day in July 2017? How did
he come to park beside, or in the vicinity of,
just that particular car? By chance? It seems
unlikely.

What made him so mad that he impulsively
cut the roof to pieces with a sharp tool? It was
totally destroyed. What drove him to that?
Who lay behind it? Did something trigger a
reaction in Mats that led to his using violence by
vandalising a car? Not a car selected by chance,
but a car whose owner he knew – and he knew
her really well.

Why did he get so angry and out of control
there and then? His thoughts must have been
completely locked into something of which we
know nothing. An intelligent man, with strat-

egy as his forte, did this openly in front of a large group of people, so there was no lack of witnesses. He was arrested by a security guard who then rang the police who handcuffed him and took him to the local station for questioning.

An interrogation with a vulnerable person who was more or less unable to speak and who was surely already in despair over how he had reacted a while earlier. He was immediately given a lawyer as his temporary defence. Everyone in the room had understood that Mats was ill. They gave him pen and paper so he could try to tell them what had happened without speaking, but that was also impossible. I have emails and texts from this final period of his life, and usually it was impossible to work out what he was trying to say even in writing.

So their contact had probably continued during the entire time he was ill. But why? And what was she doing there that day if it had not been planned? She lived a long way away, so that their running into each other, or being parked next to each other was a matter of chance, is a story I shall never believe. It must have been planned. But by whom, who wanted to have that meeting?

In July 2017 when this happened, I was away for a few days. I was able to go away thanks to our son who was still living at home that summer. He kept an eye on his dad, who was still independent and drove to see his horses every day as a rule. There were still two months left until everything fell apart, in the middle of September, when Mats was admitted to hospital as an emergency case, with urinary tract infection. Then came the final month of his life, when he was cared for in our home, when he was fed through a tube in his stomach, when he was doubly incontinent, and slept more than he was awake, and when he was assessed for his mental capacity. Back then I still did not doubt that we were soon going to move back to Sweden together. Nobody doubted it.

Consequently, from that point in July, an awful situation became a more impotent situation that tortured me. I was really anxious and realised that something drastic must be done.

It was time, and it was this that made me consider getting us away from there – where somebody had some interest in him, however totally transformed he was. He clearly did not want to tell me anything about what had happened.

For two weeks, I tried to find out what had happened. In his distress, he begged the bank to help him pay off the damages, to avoid a trial. He did this by showing the bank the email he had received from the police. I found out about this and begged him to be honest, so I could solve whatever trouble he had ended up in. I still did not know what he had done. Every day for two weeks I asked him what he had done, and in the end he showed me the email from the police on his mobile. I quickly grabbed his mobile and forwarded the message to myself. Why was somebody demanding money from him? Lots of money.

Now I was able to act and I immediately made contact with the person investigating the case. That was a relief, but a dreadful feeling all the same. The dimension we now found ourselves in was not only medical but also legal, with the risk of a trial looming up. My son and I went to the police station to meet the policeman who had conducted the interrogation. He was such a wonderful person, who immediately calmed me down by saying that we would sort this out together. If we could compensate the woman financially, then Mats would be freed, but the sum she had stated was huge. Correct perhaps, perhaps too much. But I had a hundred other things to be responsible for, so I had to exclude the possibility of investigating whether it was truthful or not. If we paid her, then the matter would be over and done with. And that was what happened. We paid the amount she demanded – but still it did not end there.

28 JANUARY 2018

When the diagnosis of frontotemporal dementia was made, I realised that I must communicate it to others than just family and friends.
It was important for example that our bank
received information about this illness that had
changed their client's personality. It was thanks
to this that I acquired the first clue that Mats
had been mixed up in something illegal. He
had made contact with the bank, via email, and
asked for a large sum of money to be transferred
to somebody's account. We had a shared bank
account, and therefore the bank rang me when
somebody unknown to the bank was to have a
large sum of money transferred into their bank
account from us. They did their duty and asked
if I knew anything about the transaction.

That was during the time I was away for a
few days. When they said the name of the person to whose account the money was destined,
I knew who it was. I lost my breath and my
thoughts flew round and round, wondering

what this was about. How could so many unthinkable things keep on happening all the time?

It was like one nightmare in the middle of another nightmare. When Mats finally confessed to me, I did what I was compelled to do. I hunted for the email addresses of the couple who were demanding money from Mats. Then I wrote to them using as few words as possible – I asked whether they were wanting to get in touch with him for some reason and whether they knew about his diagnoses. I told them which diagnoses he had and how ill he was, in the belief that there was a chance they would respond, so we could have a dialogue, but nothing happened at that point.

However, an email to Mats from the other woman's husband arrived eventually demanding further payments: *'This brings the running total of additional charges to my car to £xxxx.xx.'* The accusation was that his car tyres had been slashed on repeated occasions by somebody he believed was Mats. I did not reply, but kept in contact with the police since this was now beginning to look like blackmail: *'In the event that you pay the money above for my replacement tires within 24hrs I will not contact the police. You have until 1600hrs tomorrow. Elizabet [SIC] has the bank details.'*

What was it he actually revealed here? Apart from the fact that he could not spell my name. That he knew how ill Mats was and that it was only through me that a payment could take place, just like the compensation for the car roof. He knew in other words with certainty that Mats did not understand and therefore could not organise a bank transfer. Yet he still threatened him and was careful to copy my address into the email.

If it was true that this damage was also Mats' work, then of course it had to be proved, and it was the business of the police to investigate it. Having committed one crime does not make a person automatically guilty of another crime. We both received these threatening emails.

29 JANUARY 2018

I have read everything over and over again. And I feel so sorrowful when I see the worry in the answers that Mats can barely achieve in writing, an incomprehensible content, and the only thing that is clear is his fear. The threats of being accused again frighten him. What kind of a person writes in that way to somebody he knows is dying of ALS/FTD? The threats made it necessary for me to inform the police that Mats was being subjected to blackmail by the other woman's husband. I therefore took the step of forwarding the email that he had sent to me and my daughter at the beginning of July the year before. So seriously did I take those threats.

On 2 July 2016, we had both received the email that described details about the woman and Mats, about their planned trip and other information about Mats family. For me, it also described what that husband was like, his character and personality – his strong will and desire to damage us all – Mats, me and our children. To do anything he could out of frustration and bitterness for having been betrayed, to make me hate my husband and our children renounce their father. It felt necessary for the police to know about that. How he had treated me and wanted to revenge himself on my husband.

We paid for the damage to the car roof, for which further evidence was definitely not necessary – I do not know how many people had witnessed that scene. However, I naturally did not pay for a hypothesis that tires had time and time again been slashed by the same perpetrator. He certainly believed that he had frightened me with his threats of going to the police. Actually, however, he was doing me a service – since I had already been in communication with the police for the past weeks. I showed them the e-mails with threats and blackmail for money to pay for the slashed tires. I was relieved by the support I received and the police's professional handling of the case in cooperation with me, and their carefulness in protecting Mats. One is innocent until proved guilty, even if one has recently been on the wrong side of the law.

When the documents from the police arrived in the post, confirming that the case was closed, I showed them to Mats. He took it in slowly, and the understanding that he was out of danger of being arrested again and prosecuted came to him gradually. The grief of seeing this, apart from all that was already terrible to live with, affected me. My terminally ill husband, for whom my heart broke again and again. The evidence of how wrecked he had become and how completely vulnerable he was to anyone who wanted to hurt him. Thinking the thought of how his life would have been if he had not had my protection plagued me. Think that somebody wanted to hurt him even more than his fate had already done.

After these events, I was always on edge. Now I knew with certainty what had happened and that similar situations could arise again. He was a danger to himself and beyond normal control. He was not innocent, but he had atoned for his crime. He was gravely ill and therefore easy prey. Very vulnerable. He was quite clearly ill and I could only pray that he would not be subjected to even worse things.

Frontotemporal dementia is an unknown form of dementia, a frightening illness for those living with it and in the daily life that it brings with it. When people talk about dementia illnesses, they talk about Alzheimer's. That is important, but it is wrong to ignore other forms of dementia because they only afflict a few people. When all the people involved are counted, the few become many: family, friends, others surrounding us, his employer, the polo club, the bank and the police, to name only the few in our case.

30 JANUARY 2018

How fortunate we were to have time to meet his family and his long-standing best friend as late as a month before he died. At that time, everything was more or less as it had been for quite a while. We managed to return to England, then came his urinary tract infection and the beginning of the turn downhill. I have kept a receipt from British Airways from the last flight – the receipt for his checked-in baggage. It is still stuck in his passport – 11 September.

At the airport, he ran into a good friend and they went looking for me, finding me sitting waiting. His friend was very happy and wanted of course to talk, but Mats was unable to and so I did the talking for him. It must have been quite a long time since they had last been in contact and I saw in the friend's face that he was wondering what was happening. We exchanged email addresses and I wrote immediately and described the situation. He got worried of course, this man whom Mats knew well.

They were diagnoses that many people had never heard of. The next time I met him was at the funeral.

Two months after Mats' death, I met the professor in the ALS team. I was searching for answers and he was the one who could help me. I wanted to know as much as possible to understand. Why it ended as it did. Dying without any warning. Nobody was prepared for that, not even the doctors. I was not prepared, despite having been in the midst of everything, in the middle of all the drama. We paid an emergency visit to the healthcare centre in mid-September and then to the emergency department the day after. There he was admitted to a ward. He was admitted because I refused to take responsibility for having him at home in the condition that he was in. A condition that the hospital doctor must have considered normal for me to take responsibility for. Was that my duty? Had she even read his journal when she wanted to discharge him from the A&E? Did she have the whole picture of his illnesses clear in her mind? Who cared really that he was dementia? I have wondered about that many times.

I was a troublesome next of kin and said: 'If you consider him healthy enough to live at home in this condition then you have to know that he will be alone. I am not trained in health-care and I will not take control.' Her response was immediate: of course he could stay. It was probably clear in his journal that this patient had ALS with FTD and would not be able to live on his own, or take care of himself. Yet they still put pressure on me, as I experienced it. Did they hope that a next of kin would not oppose them but return home and continue to take the responsibility? Single-handed and alone?

After ten days, 15–25 September, Mats came home, although he was in far too bad a condition. The urinary tract infection that was the cause of his admission to hospital by the A&E doctor coincided with the planned PEG oper-ation. This is a kind of tube that leads straight into the stomach, and an operation that is com-mon for ALS patients when they can no longer get nourishment by eating normally. Swallow-

ing difficulties get worse and worse as the illness progresses.

Why – why, really, was it so urgent to determine the dementia diagnosis when there was
no plan of giving any assistance at all when it
was needed? How was that possible, when they
knew what was going to happen to his brain,
his speech and behaviour? We had no safety net
planned when the dementia became dangerous
to live with for us both. Could it even have
become dangerous for those around us? Must
I be responsible for another individual's actions
and disabilities on my own? The dementia diagnosis was established in December 2016, and
this was happening in mid-September 2017.
They had had nine months to prepare for it.

I have read the medical journal. There are
no notes on how to monitor dementia, or
when essential contacts should be put in place
for forthcoming support. Who should I turn
to, what number could I call when what was
expected to happen actually occurred? When
I could no longer control the situation with a
husband who could not look after himself and

who was helpless if he did not have somebody by his side all the time?

The ALS was followed up in minute detail, as it should have been, but it seems that the frontotemporal dementia was just something extra that we were expected to cope with on our own. Until I became a person I did not want to be, but was forced to be so as not to break down completely. If I had not made that demand, then Mats would not have been admitted to a ward following the visit at the A&E that evening on 15 September. We would not have had carers in our home when he was discharged and until he passed away. Just for a few weeks, four times a day, with a total of two and a half hours every twenty-four hours. And that was only because I refused to learn how to feed and give medicines via a PEG, because at that point I realised that help was something I had to demand. What did a decision like that do to me?

I am convinced that the routine was that both patient and next of kin had to learn this for themselves. He would not be able to handle it himself and so someone else must take responsibility for his getting nourishment. Words do not always have the same effect as actions. My action was awful, but it was the only option I had if I was to continue to provide security – the security of our being together.

The PEG and double incontinence were my limit. I knew that and I listened to myself in the midst of the chaos. I knew that by refusing to learn how to feed my husband we would be offered care at home. I am so thankful that I did. Finally, Mats' dementia was given the attention that had been denied it for nine months! My devotion and warmth could last a little longer, and I could give what I believe that I did best, what no carer could possibly replace. The closeness and calm that come from love.

31 JANUARY 2018

Our kitchen and bedroom were transformed into a nursing home. The carers came four times a day and gave Mats nutrient solution and medication via the PEG. He was no longer able to swallow his Riluzole tablets. I tried to encourage him to take his daily shower when he was no longer able himself to take the initiative. He was incredibly tired, always so tired, and I said so to the carers at every opportunity. 'It's the medicines,' they replied. I believed it, and I am sure they did too. However, later on, several weeks after the day of his death, I read about what often happens when somebody is nearing the end. Tiredness and incontinence were two things that were mentioned.

Imagine if I had known that those were signs that he was actually dying. I did not realise that – he still managed quite a lot by himself and was still mobile, although he was thin as a rake. The urinary tract infection proved to be prostate enlargement. He was given medication to address it but it made no difference. They tried another prescription but that did not change or improve anything either. All this happened one month before he died. In the late summer, he was still riding, taking his medicine himself in liquid form and coping well on his own, physically.

I was probably a horrible person. I could not take any more and manage everything on my own, at that point. For a start, Mats had received antibiotics from the healthcare centre's doctor but he did not get any better, and the day after, he awoke in a drenched bed. He had wet himself and he was confused. I rang the MND care team in desperation: 'I can't keep him at home like this, I must have help.' The reply was that someone would ring me during the day. Nobody did.

Towards evening, I decided that we would have to go to A&E. We were admitted and quickly met a doctor who looked at Mats' swollen abdomen and said that he needed to be emptied of urine. That was done and the urine that came out in great volume was heavily discoloured. A while after that, we were told that we could return home. Actually, we were not told – I was. Mats was barely conscious.

He had fallen asleep as soon as he had been freed from all the urine. He had been given a painkiller. It was at that point that I refused and said: 'If you send him home, then it will be without me, he'll have to look after himself, I can't handle it on my own anymore.' Then I said that the MND nurse had promised to ring and prepare A&E for our arrival, and that a bed would be made available in the neurological ward. I do not know if that communication had taken place, but the doctor realised that I had no intention of taking any further responsibility for Mats in the state he was in.

Why was I forced to become a monster? I only wanted the best for my desperately ill husband who could no longer speak or make himself understood in writing. He was in pain and obviously affected by the infection. Had he been living alone, I know that healthcare staff would not have discharged him. They knew that he was in danger if he did not receive help.

The dementia made him completely helpless, but they pressured next of kin because they were pressured by the system. They do a fantastic job, uphill all the way, with criticism from many directions. All the decisions, the hard labour, working overtime and being underpaid. It is easy to understand that their strength does not always stretch to doing more than resources allow. Not until there is no choice, when they find themselves in a situation with a next of kin who has become demanding and difficult, who says no, having reached her limit.

1 FEBRUARY 2018

I watched a YouTube clip from 2011, an international ALS conference at which Mats' doctor among others was giving a lecture. I do that sort of thing more and more often, having a need to remain in contact with neurology. I feel the need to understand and learn more, to be where I now belong and want to have my place. I cannot let go of it, and wonder if it would have been different if I had still been living in England. Is it because I do not have anyone here in Sweden who is linked to what we went through? Nobody here has any connection to that part of my life. It may be my way of working through my grief. I feel best when I am rooting around in everything that happened and would prefer to be there, back in the right environment.

I wanted among other things to read his journal and applied to do so. It went well and I was well received at the hospital. I was allowed to sit in a room and read it. But I was not allowed to sit alone, and had to have an admin-

istrator with me in the room. All the pages
that I wanted to take with me I marked with
post-its and the administrator copied them for
me. It amounted to about a third of the journal. Reading it has helped me even though I do
not understand everything. I can return to it
whenever I need to check something and will
always keep it with me. It is part of what I call
my medication to become whole again, and it
has had a great and positive effect on how I feel
and how I am moving on. Once again, I am not
sleeping well. I wake up, go to sleep, wake up,
go to sleep. Something has been bothering me
for some time. Do I not feel at home in Sweden? I am still not back at work, and I have not
got the children here, close to me. As my wise
son expressed it: now when we most need each
other, we happen to be living in different countries.

That's how it turned out, but that was not
the intention with the move. It was to have
been the two of us moving back together, not
just me alone. We were to have been close to
everything important during the last period

of his life. Our families, both of them. Friends from when we were growing up, friends of us both. Special relationships. That was the core of the decision we made together in July. And then Mats also had the illusion about doctors who would do something to cure him. We would not come home to better ALS care than in England, as I found out. My own referrals (an option if there is no referral from a doctor) confirmed this discovery when Swedish health-care did not respond in any way. My work would have to continue. Better ALS care than in England just did not exist. However, we had our blood ties and our histories. Not least a unique friendship between my husband and someone from his youth, his best friend of all.

2 FEBRUARY 2018

One day, a long time after Mats had died, there was a ring on my doorbell. It was an 'admirer' from Mats' time in the military, in which he must have appeared as an exemplary leader and captain. This must have been what he radiated to the young recruits, a prime example of stamina and courage. Correct to a certain degree, I believe. He did everything himself that he demanded of others. He saw himself as a von Trapp.

I could not remember Mats ever having mentioned the man who rang my doorbell. He was very courteous and explained that he was on a 'looking back' journey to people who had crossed his path and who had made a great impression on him. Mats was a person who had always left an imprint, who was either liked or disliked, and who took up plenty of space. The simple fact that this man had found me must have demanded some kind of strong ambition to achieve his goal. I could have shut the door

and refused to speak with him. He had taken
that risk. A familiar sort of behaviour indeed!
But I did talk to him so that he got to know
as much as I deemed was sufficient. Cautious
openness during a short walk.

Had Mats' years in the military contributed
to the illness? Perhaps in combination with
his ambition to practise sports at a demanding
level, in the form of skiing from heights requir-
ing a helicopter for access. Riding, especially
field competitions and polo …

*Slightly more than 200 persons in Sweden
are affected by amyotrophic lateral sclerosis,
ALS, each year. Defence staff are no exception. However, is there over-representation
among foreign veterans? After it was revealed
that three foreign veterans have been afflicted
by ALS, the Defence Force Veterans' Centre started a study to discover the status among
foreign veterans. Of a total of 2,000 Swedish
foreign veterans who have served in international theatres some time during 1990-2018,
there were eleven cases of ALS. The study*

shows that foreign veterans ran more than twice the risk of getting ALS compared with a matched control group. At the same time, the study cannot establish if there is a causal link between military foreign service and ALS in Sweden.

What causes ALS is mostly unknown, but research has progressed slightly. The majority of those affected have a combination of genetic factors and various forms of environmental impact. A person's lifestyle may also influence the risk of being affected ALS. Known so-called environmental risk factors that increase the risk of being affected by ALS are for example chemicals, head injuries, hard physical training and electromagnetic radiation. (13)

3 FEBRUARY 2018

I am disorientated in this void. Nowadays it is just me, as a widow or single; whichever term one uses, I am just me, alone. I must find my own focus and my own daily life here. Everyone else has their daily life and this 'honeymoon' will soon come to an end. At the point in time when what happened is no longer something new but just history, for everyone except me.

How long does grief last? I miss Mats and believe that we had a good relationship when we reached the parting of the ways, which would have happened even if he had lived. I think he would have found a permanent separation, ending our marriage, difficult actually — even though he seemed so strong and powerful, and nothing could stop him. But there I was the stronger. Did I give him something that he himself did not have? Something that he was unable to define, but that did him good without him knowing it?

I am back where I had to stop in October 2016. Now I want to know more and more about both illnesses, to understand and analyse. I miss the contact with the doctors and the specialist nurse. I miss them often. It seems like a desire for closeness to everyone who had responsibility for Mats, since they all understand better than anyone else what he was like during the last period of his life.

It is natural to want to remain in all we shared together, where we shared it. I read about a girl who went through a serious cancer illness when she was very young, and she was in hospital for long periods of time. When she was eventually free from treatment, she went back there, even though one may assume that that environment was the last place she wanted to be in. But it was there, in the play therapy section, that she was able to work through her thoughts.

Many of our close friends did not meet Mats during the whole time he was ill. That was just how things turned out and no accusation is implied. Some of them met him once or twice, but our existence and its ingredients were shrinking all the time. Particularly since he did not want to be with me other than on his own terms for six months, March to August 2016. That is why more words are needed to describe how everything was when people close to me have no images of him at that stage of his illnesses.

Being there in daily experiences like changes, critical situations, irritations, difficult conversations, obstacles and the demands of every single day – the wretchedness of a brain that was being damaged at breakneck speed. Seeing, hearing, living with and handling it all according to my best capacity, and with the resources to which I had access – this was our reality. My experience. The children's experience. Nobody else experienced it. Nobody knows one hundred percent what happened in our lives, what it was like to wake up every morning. However much I try to tell.

Perhaps somebody may think that I am exaggerating or being dramatic, like the occasion when I was told I should have a guardian for Mats. Or when somebody said to me that he should no longer drive a car, or that he should not have any responsibility for our finances. Neither of those things could be accomplished without some measure of cooperation from him.

Was I supposed to make that kind of cooperation possible? Although he did not cooperate in any way with me? When he kept me out of his own decisions? Should I be able to work miracles while he just went his own way? Why should solving that be a problem, it's just legal stuff, isn't it? It's just a case of sitting down, telling him the situation and asking him to see what's best for him, isn't it? I myself can almost hear how confusing it must be to get the full picture of the existence I am trying to describe. What sense can anyone make of the picture I am trying to give? That this was our life situation in reality. Is it possible for outsiders to have views? Opinions that I could have done things differently? You could have done this instead. Why didn't you contact this person or that doctor?

I actually feel very muddled when I try to relate everything. Just as when I write. Is it completely disjointed? It is perhaps just as unstructured and confusing as it was to exist in it, to live in it every day. There are so many bits and pieces, a conveyor belt of new difficulties and a complete lack of structure. Nothing is chronological or logical. Sometimes I do not know in which order I have said things, if I have said everything, to whom I have told what and how clear what I say is to the person listening.

4 FEBRUARY 2018

Riluzole was prescribed in England for him the first time in the spring of 2017. He had not wanted to take it earlier, since one has to be unmedicated if one is to be included in research. That was what he hoped so intensely for the first six months after the diagnosis. That particular doctor at the healthcare centre had never prescribed Riluzole before, and was therefore compelled to get out a catalogue of all types of medication in the UK. His spontaneous comment when he put the catalogue down was: 'It's a very expensive medication.' What did he say? Did he say what I think I heard? I believe, I hope, that Mats missed that comment. Should I have said: 'Don't worry, he won't be on it for long.' A comment on costs to a dying person, who wants to take the only medicine available to make a tiny, tiny difference in the length of his life.

I was over-sensitive to everything that felt wrong, cold, careless and unnecessary. I got angrier and angrier during the final months, until the end. My anger was concerned with wanting to do the best possible. It was essential in my struggle for Mats. If one does not get angry, then nobody listens. Raising my voice was my only weapon. Refusing certain things turned into another, like not learning to give nutrient solution or medicines via a PEG. I felt like a defender and a protector, and had more and more often a need to yell to get a reaction.

Sometimes, I could manage to keep calm and now I can manage even more. I cannot be quiet until I have done everything I possibly can. Acknowledgement and dignity to next of kin must be given more attention when somebody is living with a death sentence. Such persons must not be pressured to the point that they are close to giving up. However, one does not give up. Perhaps that is why progress is so slow? One is there. Now I want to continue to be there and to do something. That is my focus, my meaning and purpose.

If I can contribute to an improvement, if only for a handful of people, then I hope to be able to experience the feeling that everything was not in vain. In vain is the wrong term, but I cannot find a better one. It is Mats' right, my not letting go of this. Making something meaningful out of what tormented all four of us. Making a difference for other people.

5 FEBRUARY 2018

Between 12 September and 12 October I was the only person to be with Mats, along with the healthcare team. Apart from two close friends who visited us on 11 October. That means a lot to me and to them. Their errand was to sign the power of attorney that Mats had signed so that I could complete the purchase of the flat without him joining me. He seemed to understand it fairly well. So, that was on 11 October. I know that they were shocked to see how thin he was, and also moved by how he picked up the daily paper and showed them an article that he was interested in – it was in any case highlighted here and there. That visit is a fine memory for all three of us.

It was this that was so unreal, that I ponder over again and again. He had a small degree of liveliness left, some insight, an interest in reading the newspaper and interest in an article. Side by side with his dying. Concurrently – this was the day before he died. At the same moment the day after, nothing of that was left. Then he was unconscious.

A number of important memories and links to Mats are missing here in Sweden. I have to return to significant people in England, and among other things have several more conversations with my psychologist. I can talk without telling her anything particular and without explaining, while focusing on understanding, forgiving, and being reconciled to what it means to have taken care of somebody I was gradually losing. I feel desperate to get some perspective on my anguish.

I made several attempts to get help from a psychologist once I had moved back to Sweden. All three were professional and had been recommended to me, but talking to them gave me nothing. I had one or two appointments with each of them. None of them had what I was looking for – the background, but above all, thorough knowledge about the illnesses. There was only one place from which I really wanted to get help and there they said no. No, because Mats had never been their patient. The

ALS team we would have belonged to if he had lived with his illness in Sweden. One of three clinics to which I sent our own case referral. It was logical, as I realised. But it was like standing in an empty field, one that I also had to harvest myself. Therefore I chose to follow the advice of my psychologist in England. Writing became the route to acceptance, and my diary an instrument for readjusting my life.

The feeling of guilt was the first thing to sort out, a priority to be free again. The feeling of anxiety will take more time, it is linked to trust – being loved. A trust I want to be able to share with somebody, being confident in a loving relationship again. To let go of tensions around incurable illnesses and not let them take control. Drop the fear of things that can happen over which one has no control. Savour all the wonderful things in life. Capture them and the joy of living.

There was no time or need for any conversations with my psychologist towards the end, since it was doing that counted, one thing after another, and I was like a machine. Apart from contact with healthcare in England and Sweden, removal firms must be contacted and decisions about the renovation of our home must be taken. It must be new and fresh when we moved in.

Cleaners had to be booked for the house we were leaving, and the rental contract cancelled. I contacted people in healthcare concerning the acute needs I had described in our own referrals to three different healthcare units in Sweden: the healthcare centre, the ALS clinic and the dementia clinic. I took responsibility for our finances and bills and saw to it that our beloved cat was comfortable in the midst of all the muddle with people in the house the whole time, and I tried to organise a new home for him. And, a completely new assignment, that of arranging temporary care for Mats in England. To leave me free for around twenty-four hours in mid-October to travel to Sweden for the handing over of the keys.

The smallest details can make me happy now. I talked to a man while waiting for the bus. I had a lamp in a bag and it made him curious. He was an electrician, he said. I told him that I had got the wrong kind of lamp and was going back to have it changed. Then we continued chatting until the bus arrived, and he told me among other things where he had grown up and he radiated cheerfulness that gloomy winter's day.

It was such a feeling of recognition for me and just what I wanted – a bit like in England. On days when I did not socialise with anyone, I chatted with many anyway, finding time for a few minutes' light conversation that makes one come alive. Feel that one belongs with other people for a little while, instead of just standing there. It is all the more important when one lives alone, for someone to take the initiative to chat.

6 FEBRUARY 2018

Mats' writing deteriorated gradually. Sometimes it was correct and sometimes incomprehensible. It became more and more indecipherable. I sometimes received messages from friends he had written to when they did not understand at all what he had wanted to say. When I received an email like that, or a text of another kind, and saw with my own eyes sentences with two or three words, often a mixture of English and Swedish, then it became clear how the dementia was destroying his language. What thoughts were going round in his head? Was his writing worse than his capacity to think? I think so – his language did not say everything about his ability to reason. He was still functioning well, partially, in certain contexts. He was completely clear for example about all the appointments that were booked for him with the doctors. They were written down in an organised way.

What Mats was able to express in writing, in emails or texts, were short, incomplete sentences with a mixture of Swedish and English, like the following examples:

'Jag är looking at JAG!! Katten var ligger här!!' was a description of a brief moment of one day.

'Kom du,, träffa din CAR,, jag kunde HOME,,, Please you CAR,, Please,, KRAM!!' was a message about how and where we were going to meet.

'I kan,,, right ben,,, to teriffic!!' was his description of how his right leg was feeling.

'En man från ball in the face!!! En bloodies so much!!!' Here he was describing a riding accident. Somebody had been hit by a polo ball (which is made of wood) in his face and it had bled a lot.

Receiving information and instructions became harder for him, and I learned not to include too many details at one and the same time. I had instead to break it down: I'm going out shopping now; I'm going to work now for a few hours; after our appointment at the hospital we must go to the chemist's; and so on. Never more the whole flow of a long sentence, because then I saw the empty, questioning expression in his eyes. Bit by bit, morning and afternoon, day by day.

It was tricky to remember to keep one step ahead and to guess how he would react, and it was unpleasant when I did not actually manage to reach him. What shall I tell him and what shall I leave out? For his own good and our harmony, and still get everything done that must be done. It was a case of always being prepared to meet his way of taking in information.

Hugs and proof of love came in a constant flow. He hugged me not only with his arms but also with his legs. He did this often while I was busying myself in the kitchen. He would come up to me, put his arms around me and hold me as hard as he could, at the same time as he would lift up one leg and try to wind it around mine as well as he was able. I received these signs of thirst and anguish with a stab of pain in my heart. They hurt me because they were acts of spasmodic anxiety, loneliness and a repeated 'forgive me'. He devoured my closeness. He could not get enough of it.

7 FEBRUARY 2018

In August 2016, before the diagnosis was confirmed, he said: 'I don't know why I did it.' Rejecting me, that must partly have been it. Bold, drastic and sudden actions, without emotion or any link to other people, without any thought of the consequences: *'The hallmark of [Behavioural Variant] FTD is personality changes, apathy, and a progressive decline in socially appropriate behaviour, judgement, self-control and empathy.' (14)*

To some extent I have to believe that frontotemporal dementia pushed him into some of his actions, but he certainly enjoyed the kick, the power, the novelty, the joy of life, and the playing with fire. Living for the moment and taking what was on offer. Nowadays I can almost be pleased for him that he had the opportunity to experience the delicious feeling of being in love, without responsibility, and a more youthful life focusing only on himself.

I have to enjoy his enjoyment and be glad that he had vigour enough before he realised what had affected him physically – his theory about stress had faded away. However, it must never be denied that his choice hit me and the children hard. There are several kinds of grief. I read some relevant examples in books about grieving.

Mats was not alone in making a choice. The other woman also made a choice, her choice, that spilled over onto others.

8 FEBRUARY 2018

Two months after Mats' death, my daughter and I had an appointment with the professor. He explained to us what was probably the cause of the drastic deterioration that led to death. The part of the brain that controls the breathing and its regularity even when we are asleep is sometimes affected and destroyed by ALS. This was probably the cause, we were told, not that his breathing was ineffective because the capacity of the diaphragm had been weakened.

It was the system of signals that controls the rhythm of our breathing, the Pre-Botzinger complex, that stopped working as it should have done, if that is the correct way of expressing it. Therefore there was an aggressive deterioration in a very short time. Mats still had the physical strength to breathe, but the automatic system just gradually ceased to play its part. His unregulated breathing meant that too much carbon dioxide built up in his system and that also made him extremely tired and certainly also dizzy.

When he pointed towards his head with his hands it was to tell us that. If we had not been with him that morning, he would have passed away peacefully. That is the way it has been described, as peaceful – carbon dioxide narcosis.

I hope, and want to believe, that he found living in his tired world quite pleasant, and that he did not feel any anxiety or fear. Dementia may have made things easier for him by reducing the amount he was able to take in and limiting his thoughts. How can I know for certain? However, he seemed relaxed. No more anger or frustration, instead he seemed content just to sit on the sofa. He left his body and its needs to the carers and watched while they cleaned the PEG and gave him nourishment, medicines and water through it.

One of the medicines may also have contributed to his tiredness, said the professor, and the PEG operation can also sometimes cause further weakness in the patient and lead to physical deterioration. The operation wound healed well, but I wonder how much nourishment he was able to retain. His digestive system was never again stable after nutritional drinks had been introduced earlier, in June. They were initially a complement to the small amount of ordinary food he was able to eat, but towards the end they were generally speaking his only source of nourishment. We tried changing to a lactose-free variant to exclude the possibility of intolerance, but that changed nothing. The time we spent with the professor was indispensable and nice, and I saw that he really did want to explain and help us to understand. He showed great warmth and a personal understanding that I had not experienced with him in the same way earlier. Was it easier when it was all over and just us, the next of kin, there? Or was I different now that Mats was not sitting beside me? Perhaps that had an effect and made the meeting special.

Sometimes I ask myself what all those death sentences must do to a doctor. Having a job in which one can never offer any hope. However, the specialists almost certainly do not feel or think that way. They are motivated perhaps like a kind of detective – with the possibility of finding or at least contributing to coming close to a solution. Or even to solving the mystery. Research is the driving force, I believe. When it comes to ALS, there is no plan of treatment, only a plan of action.

What holds their own hopes up so that they can cope with giving terrible news to people? That they offer a certain security and some form of care within the framework that exists? But knowing with 100 percent certainty that their patients are going to die from this, most of them in just a couple of years, how do the doctors handle that? No exceptions, no improvements, just different varieties of the same thing. The illness was described for the first time in 1869, by J M Charcot, a French neurologist (15). There still seems to be a long way to go until an effective treatment exists, one that can cure or stop ALS completely. Riluzole does not do anything like that.

9 FEBRUARY 2018

How did Mats experience being dependent on me? Having to ask me to make a call for him. Pay the road tax and insurance, book appointments. Appointments with the doctors, the speech therapist, his dietician and the specialist nurse. And to be the link to his employer. It must have been awful for him, isolating and frustrating – a world that was shrinking. The same thing happened with his riding and polo. The team he belonged to for many years, a context in which I had not played any part at all before.

I am not a horsey person. Horse sports have high status, it seems, and that meant nothing to me. Therefore I have always been uninterested in that setting. I am not somebody who it is beneficial status-wise to talk to or be seen with. Suddenly, when the last season was approaching, I did play a role for Mats' well-being. I wanted the couple responsible for his riding training to know exactly how his illnesses affected him. I was keen for them to be aware of his deterioration since they last met him in the autumn of 2016. That was just before they travelled back to Argentina at the end of the polo season in England. Shortly after Mats had told them that he had ALS.

When the spring of 2017 arrived, I got to know that they wanted to have direct contact with his doctor instead of with me. If anything happened to Mats or if they had any questions, it was the doctor's word that would decide the issue, as they said to me. That made me unhappy. Why could we three not have that contact together instead? It was naive, the whole thing, not least with consideration to professional secrecy and confidentiality.

Did they believe that the professor would reason with persons who socialised with Mats through riding? That he would ring them, write and communicate during the summer about whether or not Mats would be able to compete? About possible consequences if he got injured? Mats had not lost his right to decide for himself. Would he follow advice from the doctor if it meant limiting himself? The polo team should have known him better than that. Riding, matches and tournaments had for a long time been his greatest interest.

A third party, an outsider, could not demand information about Mats, could they? Possibly if he gave his permission. I said exactly that, but did not argue with them. Let them make contact with the professor if that was their strategy for excluding me. Because that was what it was all about. I do not believe that they contacted the doctor even though I gave them name, email and telephone number. However, I contacted the doctor to get his advice. It was sage advice, centred on Mats' joy in life and the medical reality if he was injured.

I tried to sort out a way of keeping every-thing together, but lost my motivation. It was so unnecessary. The other woman had friends in that circle, and their suspicion was that my aim was to work against my husband, to punish him and try to take riding away from his life. Take away his greatest joy, while all I wanted was for him to stop competing, to stop making demands on himself and just ride for the sheer enjoyment of it and for relaxation. Not to injure himself. But the beautiful thing was that the horses did the job for us. His thin, light body was enough of a signal for them to know they had to look after him, by changing into a lower gear, keeping the tempo down compared with earlier years. Mats loved his horses – he said so often.

10 FEBRUARY 2018

I have read Ulla-Carin Lindquist's book *Rowing Without Oars* in both Swedish and English. It is gripping, beautiful, sorrowful, explanatory and a great comfort and help to me. Just as the documentary about her: *Min kamp mot tiden* ('my race against time') by Andreas Franzen, who followed her during her period of illness, is of profound value to me.

I learn a lot and receive confirmation for many things. I find words and descriptions that I can identify with and that stay with me. For me, the strongest sentence is this: *'At Christmas one may make a wish, and I know what I can't get enough of: closeness, warmth, truth and trust'* (*Rowing Without Oars*, page 195) (16). Words that express everything that Mats expressed with his body, with his hands and with his eyes. It was the true meaning of these words that was confirmed for me in the room at the doctor's in Switzerland. Trust, truth, warmth and closeness. All of those were present in that room the whole time we were there. It was gripping and thought-provoking and something I shall always bear with me.

The second time that Mats visited the hospital in Switzerland, I was with him. It was then that he had read about quinine and received an explanation that he accepted. Immediately after our appointment we had to go to a pharmacy, hand in the prescription for Riluzole and preferably receive the medicine straight away. It was the only measure that could influence the course of the illness, check its speed straight away – the straw he was grasping at late in the day. The one medicine that he had not yet tested. In the hope that something real, something else, would make him healthy again, he had previously chosen not to take it. We found a pharmacy in the vicinity of the hotel we were staying at, and he rushed up to the counter and handed over the prescription. The medicine was not in supply – it had to be ordered, but we could collect it the day after. He took that information quite calmly, but the day after, when we came back he asked for a glass of water so that he could take the first tablet then and there. I can still not get close to what was going on inside him then. How did he feel and what did he expect that the effect of the medicine would be? *'Although there is no cure for ALS, Riluzole can extend a patient's survival by three to six months.'* (17) Did he realise yet that he was going to die of that illness? I have a strong suspicion that he never took it in. Instead of research, that medicine was now going to make him healthy again.

Then we had a nice day. The spring sun was shining and we walked around looking at buildings, went into shops and sat out of doors and drank coffee. I have some wonderful photos from that day. He looked healthy, suntanned and content, and I am sure that he was harmonious. I made a video when we had dinner that evening – his face was well-rounded without any sign of weight loss. He laughed and pulled faces. May I always be able to keep that film.

The day after, we flew home and the day after that it was time for another follow-up with the doctor in England. Not the same doctor as previously, but since there were two professors in the MND team, I had asked to change to the other one. Mats did not seem comfortable with the first one and that affected me too. I wanted to do what I thought he would have done if he had been able to. Important and a good thing, I thought. How wrong I was. There was no difference at all, since the second one could not offer a cure either, or participation in research. What I as his partner valued in that meeting lacked relevance. With the help of my psychologist, that was something I only realised afterwards: *'It only made a difference to you but for Mats everything was the same. He didn't get what he desperately wanted. Somebody who could promise to cure him.'*

11 FEBRUARY 2018

The day before Mats died, he was more tired than usual. I still did not know that this was a warning signal. Since he had been in hospital from 15 to 25 September, and had been discharged with the PEG, doubly incontinent and with prostate problems that were being treated with medicine, he no longer dressed himself. He walked about in his dressing gown for the most part every day, and slept on the sofa or in his bed most of the time.

What I wish is that I had known more. What could I have done if somebody had talked to me about death? What could I have done better for us both? Talked about all our shared memories? Lain beside him there on the sofa, just to be close to him? Slowed down the tempo of any plans? The whole business of moving back to Sweden, that I was having to organise alone.

I was supposed to travel to Sweden and take the final formal steps in the purchase of our flat – meet the agent and the seller to make the final payment and acquire the keys. Beforehand, in July when the purchase was agreed, our thought was that we would do the whole thing together. At the end of August, the plan was still realistic. Mats did not yet have a PEG and was thus not being tube-fed. He did not have incontinence protection and dressed himself every morning. He slept at night but not most of the day and his breathing supplied him with sufficient oxygen. Only a few weeks later, our situation was completely changed and our home had become his care home.

Who would be responsible for him for the twenty-four hours that I would be away? I could not leave him on his own, that would not be at all safe. What would he do if someone rang the doorbell and discovered the condition that he was in? What would he do if there was a fire? If an alarm went off? If there was a power cut? If he swallowed something and it went down the wrong way? If he slipped in the shower? He couldn't ring, speak or write a message. The carers would of course have come four times that day as usual – but only for about two hours. There were 22 more hours when he would have been alone!

In my desperation as time passed, I sent an email to close friends and asked if anyone was able to stay in our home while I was away. Clearly it was too much to ask. None of them had lived with that situation, and many had not even met Mats for a long time. I realised their anxiety and dilemma over taking responsibility at that level. Would I myself have been able to do that even, if anyone had asked? However, I was not functioning properly, was no longer thinking rationally, and I was desperate. Imagine if I had just left and later rung the hospital or the healthcare centre GP, and said: 'For your information, Mats is at home alone.' It would have been neither criminal nor illogical of me to have done that. What would they have done then? A quick, emergency decision about temporary care? Nobody stated the truth, that he was no longer capable of living on his own. It seemed as though only I was able to speak openly about that. Did nobody else want to see the reality? A terrible thought that Mats would be alone, without protection from somebody else, as his condition definitely demanded.

12 FEBRUARY 2018

I asked the company who employed our care team (hired by the NHS) if their help could be increased for one or two days. The answer was no, there were no resources for care round the clock even for twenty-four hours. I then rang the ALS team at the hospital and put the same question to them. There I was told that since Mats was not classed as an emergency case, he could not be admitted to hospital again. Not even the hospital where he had recently been a patient for ten days. Instead I was informed that I would have to arrange private so-called respite care myself. Yet another responsibility, and area of concern, just a few weeks before our move to the flat which first had to be renovated.

I visited a private care home that I thought seemed good and in any case I had neither the time nor the energy to look at any others for comparison. This one was close to our home. It felt like a relief and I said to the manager of the home that I wanted to book a place there for Mats for one or two days in mid-October. I thought that was all that needed to be done, if there was a room free then. And also of course that she must be in contact with the ALS team at the hospital to exchange medical information.

Clearly, it was not that simple. Before the home could accept him, an investigation had to be carried out, including a home visit. It was to assess what we all knew already – that he could not be left alone any longer, or make sound decisions for his own good. I found out that an assessment by a psychologist was required, to have grounds for the need of care round the clock, if he did not himself give his consent to it. Having to go through all this and have more anxiety and stress when a simple solution would have been to allow the carers, whom he already accepted and liked, to live in our home for at least one twenty-four-hour period. That was all I asked for.

At the same time as this was happening, I was doing the same thing in Sweden, making a care plan. However, there it was a case of per-manent care that would be required from the very first day we moved in. I had already started the care needs investigation in July, when we bought the flat. I had found out that one can write self-referrals to healthcare providers. I wrote three: one to the healthcare centre where we would be listed, one to the ALS team at the hospital to which we would belong, and a third that I hoped would meet the care needs related to frontotemporal dementia.

The dream of Sweden had nothing to do with getting better healthcare. I was aware that my struggle for Mats' best interests would be similar to the one I was already in the middle of. How long would I have the stamina to live with him in our new home? If we had access to the same home healthcare as in England, perhaps it would work out for a while? And then a while longer. Our needs would just get more and more extreme. Where was the limit? When is enough enough?

Now we only had a few weeks left until our removal van was due to take our property to Sweden. The flat must be painted and the craftsmen were going to start immediately after the handing over of the keys. They had a period of at most four weeks, and there must be no delays, because we were due to move into the flat in mid-November. An international move with a fair amount of logistics to sort out.

13 FEBRUARY 2018

On Tuesday 10 October 2017, we had an appointment to investigate Mats' mental capacity. The carer arrived as usual in the morning and gave him his medicine, nutrient solution and water. Then it was time to get dressed and ready. It went very slowly, but I was patient and said nothing to hurry him up. If we were late, we were late. Anyway, assessing him like this was so wrong to me. And 48 hours later, on Thursday 12 October, just how wrong it was, was a fact. That day was his last.

The carer mentioned above had followed my going round in circles to find a solution, had seen and interpreted that I was incredibly worried about the decision concerning the day I would not be at home but in Sweden. In the middle of October. This exceptional young man was doing a job that few were able to do in the way that he did. What warmth and care he gave us both every day, those weeks we had at home together before the end was at hand. His contact with Mats was unsurpassable – he was there for him completely and with full respect, responsibility, cheerfulness and competence. He saw my desperation and said: 'I'll stay here, you go and do what you have to do and I'll stay here with Mats.'

Which even today I think must have been a private decision and something he wanted to do when healthcare had said no. My relief was indescribable and my thoughts about the formal responsibility that he took upon himself did not come until afterwards. However, his help was never needed. I received the keys to our new flat as planned, on 16 October.

Mats died two days after the psychologist had interviewed him. She had shown him pictures of the care home and tried to penetrate into his world, to find out if he would accept being there for a day and a night.

It was an elegant report in a folder, a professional requirement with endless words that everyone needed except me, and beloved Mats. It had to exist for the sake of the system, I realise that, but still cannot understand how it is possible for that to be the routine. Everything in it, we knew already. The patient was a recognised case, and the type and extent of care needed for twenty-four hours were also well known and in place on a smaller scale.

On 10 October, a psychologist came to a conclusion. It was nothing new but necessary medically, ethically and legally. The conclusion was, among other things:

> *[...] this has resulted in significant cognitive and behavioural change consistent with behavioural variant Fronto-Temporal Dementia. Mr [...] also has significant communication difficulties due to severe dysarthria. [...] He was clearly confused about the nature of the assessment [...].*
>
> *Assessment outcome.*
>
> *Can Mr [...] understand the issue under the consideration and the information given? No.*
>
> *Can Mr [...] weigh up the information and use it to make a decision? No. He did not indicate, for example, that being alone would pose any risk to his health and safety.*

Why could I not just be given support and stability instead? Being with Mats and providing greater harmony and tenderness, as we both needed. I can dream about an end with more of that, and believe that then we would have had a chance of deeper closeness. How did he himself experience all that? Being investigated and answering hypothetical questions, with the aim of taking a stand on things he perhaps could not manage to sort out in his thoughts, when all he wanted was to rest and sleep. Some kind of care home would soon have been the next step, respite care or no respite care. I could cope no longer. When neither bladder nor bowels were working any longer, then the limit had been reached. A normal limit, I think. And the dementia was running an aggressive course and it was distressing to be solely responsible for his actions. The deterioration was out of control. One should never have to give care in that way. The last period in life must be about spiritual contact and the possibility of keeping one's integrity, being entirely present.

14 FEBRUARY 2018

I knew that paralysis would break down what was left of our strength in both of us. We rented a home. It would have to be fitted out for Mats' various needs if we remained. Would that have been approved? A care home full time would be required one day. The needs connected to dementia, in particular, would determine when. So we would have had to go through all that soon, but to do it for one day's respite care was wrong. Besides, everyone knew what had happened before the diagnosis: that Mats had met another woman and left me (just testing life apart, as he said).

I had looked after my husband during the whole course of the illnesses, starting just before the diagnosis of ALS was confirmed. Instead of running away. I feel even so that this did not count. Imagine if he had been living alone. Whose is the responsibility then, in a case like this? His own, or society's? When one had started the care process, as a next of kin, it was not easy to find support or care interventions when one had reached one's limit. But if I had never begun?

Where was she now, the woman who had previously been so valuable to him? Was she by his side at the doctors' appointments to which I was not invited? Would she have been there if I had backed away? Or was he of no value when he was no longer healthy? What I did for Mats was central for me. Knowing he was with me, and that he perhaps experienced happiness, is my road back to harmony and the joy of life. That is my foundation when looking ahead. That is soothing for my heart in the midst of my grief.

What are the children thinking? What is most painful? How great is their feeling of loss, anguish and anger? Was I even a support for my children during the time of Mats' illness? Has my love been enough, then and afterwards? I was perhaps too engulfed by myself and unable to take in their pain and feelings fully. I try to stop judging and just gradually accept. And confess that this consideration only rose to the surface when things were no longer so over-flowing and chaotic inside me.

My process was mostly about days and nights, moments and situations that were challenges to me. It stretched my entire personality and repeatedly tested my limits. Memories of distance and rationality in which I did not always have the power to be warm and show empathy for Mats' convulsively holding onto life, and onto me. In his efforts to save himself.

What was our everyday life like while Mats was alive? Did he experience any quality of life? We were angry, all four of us – parallel to feelings of love, loneliness and many mixed reactions that tormented us. We expressed them and showed them in different ways. When I read about advice now, afterwards – how to create a secure environment in a case of dementia – I know that my behaviour was not balanced. How could it have been? When one becomes everything to a gravely ill and dying person, when healthcare for dementia is absent? Invisible.

How might it have been? If I had remained in England – close to the children, an open door, to be able to look in at any time, stay a night or just have dinner. Instead, I had moved to a small town in Sweden, where we had no shared history. Their parental home was snatched away, and thereby also the security it gave, when nothing would have been better than closeness. Our missing geographic togetherness. How has that affected the children? And how has it affected me?

15 FEBRUARY 2018

Wednesday 11 October 2017 was a fine day in its way. We hugged each other for a long time when we met in the hall. One of those extralong hugs that we stood there just enjoying. And which made me feel really convinced and satisfied over what I had the ability to give. I felt Mats' peace and happiness inside me. We were one. That moment will remain with me forever. I felt his bony body, his longing and his need for it to be us despite everything, which he had clearly shown since the time of the diagnosis.

Later when he was lying resting, I stroked his cheeks and asked if he wanted anything – 'cheese cake', he tried to say. He loved cheese cake. I could only guess at what he was saying, so he had to write it down. He wrote that word absolutely correctly and I still have that piece of paper. Understandable writing was exceedingly rare by then. I went shopping and then made tea for him. He ate the whole cake, slowly, slowly, in tiny bites. It was soft and he was able to swallow it without any problem. He enjoyed it so. An intimate memory.

That evening he went to bed early as usual, at about 8.30 p.m. or so. I was sitting in an armchair watching TV, with the cat lying on the sofa. Suddenly I heard Mats getting up, and he came slowly down the stairs. It scared me because he normally slept so deeply and did not usually get up like that. He was holding onto the banister, as he had done for some time. One of his legs had started to hurt and was tender which meant that he limped. He sat down on the sofa with his dressing gown on, red socks and his traditional-style indoor slippers. I asked how he was feeling. He put his hands to his head, then lifted them up and down towards his head again, as if to say that it was heavy, that he was tired and weak, as I now believe. We sat there for a short while in silence. I remember looking down at his legs and thinking how fine and whole he was still looking, despite everything. I was very tense inside; I was afraid that something would happen and felt more and more often fear of the nights. I had a sense of being more vulnerable and alone then. After a while, he went upstairs again and slept peacefully.

16 FEBRUARY 2018

The morning after, I was unable at first to make contact with him. I caressed his face with my hand while I said: 'Mats, you must wake up now, the carer is coming soon.' No reaction, but I could clearly hear him breathing. I went down into the kitchen.

When I came up again, he was not in his bed, and I opened the door to the bathroom. He stood there with his back to me, and I said something like: 'Are you going to take a shower now?' Then he turned round and just looked at me. I thought it was a sign that he was as usual, as he had been the previous days. I went downstairs again, then up, to see to him, and he had gone to sleep again.

When the carer arrived at eight, he gave Mats his medicine and nutrient solution up in the bedroom. The next time I went up, Mats was sleeping deeply. I wanted to get some kind of contact with him, because this day had started differently. There was no reaction, and that second I realised that something threatening was now happening. The two first care visits in the mornings were close together. When the carer walked through the door for the second time, at 10.30 a.m., I told him that something was not right. He took a quick look, then came the words: 'We need an ambulance.'

17 FEBRUARY 2018

Mats lived for one year after the diagnosis. He was twice doomed – but my perspective was longer, anyway. There was the possibility that he seemed physically to be a kind of exception. However, at the same time I knew that bulbar ALS/FTD is the most aggressive combination.

He was given all available emergency help to get going again. First at home, by the carer who was instructed by emergency services over the phone while they made their way to us. Then by the team of ambulance men, and later in the hospital. I talked to him and held him tightly, and said in his ear again and again: 'I'm here, Mats, I'm right here with you.' Despite the chaos that day, I can only admire the compassion I was given, and remember especially the doctor responsible at A&E.

At about three o' clock, they said that they could not do any more for him. The children and I went with the doctor to a room nearby for next of kin. He said that the end was close and he was explicit and warm, although I felt that he was also stressed. Under pressure from his job with far too many patients to hurry away to. He said: 'It might be days, it might be hours or minutes.' What stuck with me was 'days'.

Mats looked peaceful after all the electrical cords and needles had been taken away. He was given drugs to make him relaxed and pain-free. It was quiet after the staff at A&E had said that the end was near. And restful when Mats was transferred from the A&E to the neurology ward. Exactly the same room as he had occupied in September. The still and comforting atmosphere continued for the rest of the afternoon and during the evening until he passed away with me by his side. Just before midnight on 12 October 2017. Fifty-five weeks after we had been given the diagnosis.

It was upsetting and at the same time strangely calming to see how well he was sleeping. Everything in the room was still and quiet. I caressed his face with my hand and continued talking to him. My face against his cheek. Again and again I whispered in his ear. I stroked his body with my hand. Stroked his feet. I cried with the pain of knowing how hard he had battled to conquer the illness. Did he hear or understand my words that day? That's what they say to next of kin, that hearing is the sense that remains to the end. If that is true, it is a gift, and if not, it is in any case what I want to hold onto and believe. I stayed with him for a long while – the loss was immediate and intense. Our life together was forever at an end.

A nurse came into the room at regular intervals. She gave me some tea. She held me. She gave me the time I needed. It was hard to leave, a decision knowing that I would never see him again. When I was ready at last, the nurse asked me if I had everything with me. She went over to the bed and saw that he had a ring on his finger. She took it off and gave it to me. It, and a pair of socks, were his only belongings that day.

When I was standing at the door later, ready to leave, I turned round and went back to the bed. I was in a dilemma about when it was time to leave him. Saying farewell, taking the step out of the room, to be forever finished with that last moment. But then I just had to make that decision. When I came out into the corridor, the nurse gave me a form with information. *Bereavement*, the heading read. I folded it, without bothering to read it. I had no idea what would be the next step after all the medical issues, which were what I knew something about by that time. A new and unknown field of activity – the legal.

22 FEBRUARY 2018

I tell myself that I must appreciate the good things that were part of our reality while he was ill. That will be like counting on the fingers of one hand. Five things stand out. Mats did not become paralysed; he had a strong body despite his BMI only being 18, and therefore he still had his body language even when his speech disappeared. He went riding all summer, which had always been his great joy and probably the only times when the illness did not exist in his world. He could still eat some things, though only minimally and despite his difficulties in swallowing. He was at home and remained living at home throughout his illnesses, although he died in hospital. And we had twelve additional and unforgettable hours together. The children came to the hospital in time to say farewell to their father. And I was close to my husband when he drew his last breath. I do not know how many times I have repeated all this to myself.

I have this image of him riding at a gallop – the feeling of freedom and enjoyment of being one with nature, on his beloved horses. His words had left him, but I knew what he was trying to tell me and so desperately wanted to express. His eyes, his face and his whole body still spoke to me. He showed his need for love continually, and his need for hugs was ever-present. They were firmer, longer and more intimate than ever before. He did what he could to say sorry. Those are powerful memories of which I must treasure.

In my grief, I often wanted to talk to our children. I repeated what had happened, and my thoughts about it, how I had dealt with it and how often I had experienced anguish over Mats' desperation. A despair over retroactively doing what was best. I gradually took in that they did not want to have long discussions or extended chats about all the details. I was starting to become a nag. I was repeating myself. I kept returning to what it was that was tormenting me and I was selfish in my need to reason with somebody who knew the background and had the whole truth.

When we three were on a trip together, they brought the subject up with me. I listened. I started to see that I could influence our fine times together negatively and wear out the subject with the risk of dragging us all back to a phase that we were not really still in. We had taken several strides forward. But I continued to go back. Perhaps that was my way of forgiving myself? By forcing myself into the memories that cut me to bits? The children did sometimes want to talk, but not for as long or as in-depth as I did. I got going and did not stop when they had had enough. After that conversation, I became aware of my responsibility to respect their limits, their endurance and their need of a new way of being together.

A family with three individuals, a shared experience and with individual recovery and personal healing. When one shares something, one is not best for each other the whole time. Some part of the journey must take place alone, sometimes with the help of a guide or psychologist. Somebody from the outside who can offer a sharper focus and a healthier approach.

The guilt that one is carrying around with one is easier to talk about and let go of in a room in which one is not met by personal feelings or values. Then there is space to enter into the darkness to find a way back to the light and look more clearly at one's own, often divided feelings. Then we can lovingly and in restful acceptance have Mats inside ourselves, in a place in our lives where we will always be there for each other.

26 FEBRUARY 2018

I wish that groups like carers would go on strike for a whole day, in an entire country. What chaos and what a desperate situation would result. Apart from the wrong people being affected, the message to the decision-makers and others would be clear.

When I got to know four fantastic young carers who took over our home with respect, cheerfulness and consideration, my eyes were opened to this forgotten group of professionals. Their shift started at eight in the mornings and ended after eight in the evenings. We got to know each other and I asked all kinds of questions about their job.

Among other things, I got to hear that they were not paid for the time it took them to get from one care recipient to another. Only the time from their home to the first care recipient and then from the last care recipient back home after the end of their working day. Could that possibly be the case, or had I misunderstood?

The nature of the job was that it was mobile healthcare – visiting several care recipients each day. The time between visits was thus paid for by the employees themselves, including the cost of petrol. It sounded like a full-time job, but actually not all the hours were paid for. How was that possible? Was their work not worth more? When for us it was more than indispensable. A couple of hours a day. How long would that be sufficient?

One picture I have in my inner eye is when Mats is sitting on the sofa, receiving his nutrient solution and medicines via the PEG. He is sitting there eating sweets, which had become a habit, since his need for sugar was great. It is one of the signs of that illness. He bought English chocolate – Galaxy – but also Haribo. He bought them, and I threw the Haribo away.

He ate a Haribo sweet, and it went down the wrong way. I got alarmed. It scared us all. He coughed and struggled to get the bit out that had got stuck in his throat. The carer and I both reacted immediately and did what we could to help him. The bit came up, thank goodness.

The second after it had landed in the sofa, Mats put it back in his mouth. At that point it was even more evident how badly he was functioning and how far the dementia had progressed. Not even a child would put a sweet back in its mouth that had caused a feeling of suffocation and frightened it the moment before, would it? Think what might have happened if Mats had been alone at that moment? Imagine if I had just gone out with the rubbish and a neighbour had stopped for a chat for a few minutes? *Imagine if* scenarios abounded.

1 MARCH 2018

'I'm battling on every day', as Mats often repeated. And that he did without doubt; he really did battle on every day, from morning to evening. That phrase 'battle on' in relation to *not giving up the battle, or not losing the battle to the illnesses*, is something I find difficult. Who decides what it is to battle on, and how it should be done? A certain optimism, if it is at all possible, I believe can have significance for how one lives while one is ill. I think it can have an effect on the will and ability of friends and one's surroundings to be in contact and be close.

But then what does it mean, to 'battle on' when one is seriously ill? Is it the same as regaining one's health, or living for a long time with the illness one has? Does the same kind of reasoning exist when small children get a serious illness – that the one who survived battled on, while others gave up? In my opinion, this is a cruel way to reason about and judge other people, their fate, possibilities and death. ALS is not one illness, there are several types and all of them are incurable. The average time somebody can live from diagnosis is said to be three to five years. But some people live with ALS for ten, twenty or thirty years.

If the *battle on* reasoning is also applied to ALS, then Mats has been the least successful of all. He only did it for 389 days. For me, he was and continues to be an impressive fighter. I admire how he got up every morning, had breakfast, took his medicines, showered, read the newspaper, continued to follow current affairs, hunted for a cure, had a siesta, watched TV, polished his shoes and boots, washed the car, went to the barber's for a haircut, went out for a walk, and, not least, rode his beloved horses the whole summer in 2017. That is what I consider action – against the current, not with it. My darling Mats, you did all you could and never gave up. And those were the words I chose for the beautiful ribbon round the urn. Your struggle, your not giving in. The truth about a life that was very suddenly put out anyway.

50% of ALS patients die within 18 months after the diagnosis. Only 20% are still alive after 5 years, and only 10% are alive as long as 10 years. In most cases, ALS patients die peacefully and without pain, many times in their sleep. Death is caused most often by inadequate oxygen supply, which leads to a too high level of carbon dioxide in the blood. Carbon dioxide has a narcotic effect that makes the patient sleepy. (18)

3 MARCH 2018

It was natural to organise the funeral, since it was necessary directly after his death. It was simple to make decisions for everything concerning that day. The limbo in which one finds oneself gets filled up with these tasks in a strange way. I knew exactly how things would be. Loss. Painful loss. Grief and missing him. When one has just entered into the state of *grieving*, the funeral offers an initial focal point. One needs the tasks that it demands of one. One is given the opportunity of creating memories and deciding what is most suitable. From the obituary, the church, the words, flowers, music, colours, and onwards to how everyone should gather together afterwards. It turned out well, it was honest at any rate, which was so important to me. I remember almost everything. I had listened to the music again and again and knew that it was right. Our love and the life we had shared were the centre of attention, just as they should have been, in the church that was the right place for us all.

The burial demanded more of me. It was more final, eternally significant. Even a long time afterwards, when life has moved on and grief has found its place in it. I do not really need a place to go to, or a stone to decorate with flowers and candles. Mats' place is where I am, when I want to be with him. When I want to think about him and highlight all the good things in our life. Without erasing what was not. I need to share life with him through fine memories and respect for how everything started. How we came together.

He had to have a resting place somewhere, as it's called. According to the law, one has a year at one's disposal, during which the burial must take place, as I was told by the church warden. I considered the church where we held the funeral, his childhood church, and the church next to our – my – new home. For many reasons, none turned out to be right. Time passed, until the most obvious solution matured into being.

I came to think of the region that Mats had fallen in love with when he first came to Skåne, which included the church where we got married and where our children were christened. I went there and sat outside before going in. Contemplated and adored the setting. There in that place, the choice was simple, based on his historical and romantic side. That medieval church that he had chosen for us became my choice for him.

5 MARCH 2018

While I am waiting and waiting for acceptance for how everything turned out, and working through my divided feelings and thoughts about inadequacy, I must also think of ways of hauling myself forward.

I did not kick a man who had fallen to the ground, I helped him up, forgave him and was together with him in everything that became his life as somebody incurably ill. I stayed at his side and gave all I could to create some sort of way of life in the midst of the uncertainty and the aggressive deterioration.

I did all that I had the capacity and energy to do. Through human love and respect for his very best – convinced of being there for him, loving him, protecting him. Convinced of the value of being able to forget what I must forget and preserve what strengthens our ties, to continue a harmonious life. I am going to look after our future as best I can – the children's and mine. Thank you, my beloved, for everything that was beautiful between us, thank you for our being together when you closed your eyes – with your hand in mine.

*At the end of the day, your feet
should be dirty, your hair messy
and your eyes sparkling.*

— Shanti

FROM FIRST SYMPTOMS TO DEATH

- March/April 2015 – first symptom with impaired speech

- October 2015 – initial doctor's appointment at the healthcare centre

- November 2015 – doctor's appointment at the healthcare centre

- December 2015 – referral to speech therapist (speech & language therapy)

- February 2016 – appointment with neurologist MRI scan

- February 2016 – doctor's appointment at the healthcare centre

- March 2016 – doctor's appointment at the healthcare centre

- May 2016 – doctor's appointment at the healthcare centre

- June 2016 – doctor's appointment at the healthcare centre

- July 2016 – referral to ENT specialist – appointment mid-August

- August 2016 – referral by ENT specialist to another neurologist

- September 2016 – appointment with neurologist no 2 – probably 1/9

- September 2016 – referral to lung specialist – appointment 7/9

- September 2016 – referral to lung X-ray

- 19 September 2016 – MND team's professor confirms diagnosis

- November 2016 – appointment with neurologist in Switzerland

- 1 December 2016 – clinical psychologist confirms frontotemporal dementia

- January 2017 – Mats sends blood test to neurologist in Sweden

- April 2017 – second visit to neurologist in Switzerland. Riluzole prescribed

- April 2017 – initial home visit of nurse specialist in neurology

- May 2017 – Riluzole prescribed by healthcare centre's doctor in England

- June 2017 – diverse tests and doctor's appointment at the respiratory medicine unit

- June 2017 – visit MND nutrition clinic

- July 2017 – home visit by nurse specialist in neurology – follow-up from April

- August 2017 – visit MND clinic – specialist nurse and home healthcare

- September 2017 – doctor's appointment at the healthcare centre – urinary tract problems

- September 2017 – acute urinary tract infection, admitted to hospital for 10 days

- 21 September 2017 – operation – PEG

- 25 September till 12 October 2017 – home care 2 ½ hours a day

- 12 October 2017 – Mats died in hospital just before midnight

Apart from this, Mats was regularly followed up by the professors in the ALS team, about every other month. For a few months, he had speech training at home, including mapping and advice about possible aids. The MND (ALS) specialist nurse was always available to us, with all our issues and all our questions. Without her and her warm, professional support, our daily life would have been impossible. She and Mats had a very good relationship, and her presence was meaningful for him in many ways – not least by creating trust in what was planned for him.

REFERENCES

I have chosen to include medical texts on some pages in the book where I think they clarify things. The illnesses are extremely rare and completely unknown to many. I learned a lot about the purely medical aspect but I do not pretend to have any knowledge of neurology. The text in references 1–15, 17 and 18 comes from various homepages.

ALS Association (www.alsa.org)

ALS News Today (www.alsnewstoday.com)

Alzheimer's Society – United Against Dementia (www.alzheimers.org.uk/about-dementia/types-dementia) Demensförbundet (www.demensforbundet.se)

MND Association (www.mndassociation.org) Neuroförbundet (www.neuro.se) Socialstyrelsen – Sällsynta hälsotillstånd (www.socialstyrelsen.se)

Svenskt Demenscentrum (demenscentrum.se)
The Association for Frontotemporal Degeneration (www.theaftd.org)

Ulla-Carin Stiftelse (www.ullacarinstiftelse.se)
Wikipedia

16. *Ro utan åror*, Ulla-Carin Lindquist. 2004:
Norstedts förlag Stockholm, fjärde trycknin-
gen. ISBN 91-1-301332-7

(*Rowing Without Oars*, Ulla-Carin Lindquist.
English translation: Margaret Myers. 2005:
John Murray. ISBN 0-7195-6687-8)